Abba House & Me

Prayer Changes Everything

Anne Samson

Abba House & Me: Prayer Changes Everything
by Anne Samson

Printed in the United States of America

ISBN 9781628398915

www.xulonpress.com

TABLE OF CONTENTS

ACKNOWLEDGEMENTS

First and foremost, I have to thank my family. My husband was patient and understanding as I pursued my dream of finishing and publishing this book. I am extremely grateful to my sons, particularly my older son, who allowed me to share the family experiences described in these pages. On occasion, I have doubted the wisdom of sharing so much detail about our family difficulties, and I talked to my older son about the judgments that some people in our culture make regarding mental illness. He smiled at me and said "Mom, I don't think the type of people who read your book will be making those judgments." In addition, I am also grateful to my parents, who gave me life and love, and supported us during all times, including the ones in this book. And thanks to all of my extended family, especially Aunt Florence, who has always loved us so well.

I have some special friends who were instrumental in the book's completion. Flo prayed me through the tough spots, when it seemed like every force of nature rose up to prevent me from finishing: she told me it would serve the Lord in great ways and I believe her. Sister Rose Marie provided editorial assistance, historical information, and the invaluable perspective of having lived in the original Abba House community, as well as loving, prayerful support as I wrote (and great massage!). My current spiritual director, Sister Bernice, provided spiritual common sense and great empathy. Pat was also a great encourager, with prayer and a good laugh always at the ready. My gratitude goes to Betty Ann, Maggie, Terri, Connie, Deanna Rose, Jeremy, Fran and my other "readers" as I progressed through the process of creating the book. I am grateful to everyone who provided information about the House through interviews and meetings, providing valuable insight into the ministry of Abba House. And thanks to all my wonderful friends, especially my "arm-holders" who prayed me through!

I would also like to thank Joyce Meyer, with whom I do not have a personal relationship, but whose ministry I support and benefit from tremendously. I am greatly blessed by her teachings, which help me to stay accountable and always growing as a Christian.

Finally, a special, loving thank you to Heather Haskins, who edited with skill and grace.

Prayer, from the Renovated Abba House, May 2009

I sit here and think about all the prayers
that were sent to You from this house:
from thousands of people, there were millions of prayers.
The rooms reverberate with holy energy.
It is a hope-filled place because prayer is ever hopeful.

When we connect with You in prayer
we are consoled, redirected, encouraged, and sent out again
to try our best to be your hands and feet.
So many people came to Abba House and rested with You
for a short or long while—always just enough.
I know I did.
We were changed in Your presence
and in the presence of each other.

So I write about this House of Prayer
and the women who lived it,
but they would be the first to say it is Your story, Lord.
Thank you for the privilege of telling it.

While I was researching and writing this book, I grew to know my friend and first spiritual director Sister Elizabeth Hoye, RSCJ, far better than I knew her when she was alive. She continues to speak to me from heaven in new and creative ways, less tangibly than when she lived at Abba House and then at Kenwood, but clearly nonetheless. To those of us who knew her, Sister Libby lives in our hearts forever.

When my husband read the first draft of my manuscript for this book, he asked me "What are you trying to do here?" After much thought, prayer and editing I decided that, in this book, I am attempting to:

- Write a testament to the love, care and prayer of my first spiritual director, Sister Libby Hoye;
- Recognize and celebrate the significant ministry of Abba House of Prayer and its founders, Sister Libby and Sister Mary Gen Smyth;
- Give God glory and Abba House gratitude for helping me to grow both spiritually and emotionally;
- Show others by my own experience that God walks with us through our darkest times and that He will never leave us nor forsake us;
- Acknowledge that ***prayer changes everything!***

Prologue—The End and the Beginning

Well done, good and faithful servant. Matthew 25:21a

Where do I begin?

Perhaps at the end...

Sister Elizabeth (Libby) Hoye, RSCJ (Religious of the Sacred Heart of Jesus), died on my birthday, September 3, 2007. Her death was not unexpected. After all, she had lived for nearly eighty-seven years. Sister Libby was born on December 7, 1920. I never had any difficulty remembering her birthday because my older son was also born on December 7 (Pearl Harbor Day). And so our births and deaths were intertwined, as were our lives.

When Sister Libby died, I had just started a new job as a third grade head teacher of emotionally disturbed children at a day treatment facility. I already knew that the job was not a good fit for me, and was considering resigning. In fact, after seven years of teaching, I was thinking about leaving the profession altogether, to return to government contracting and communications, where I had worked for fourteen years prior to teaching. Sister Libby had been one of my greatest supporters during my venture into teaching. During the months following her death, as I reflected on the role she had played during that part of my life, it almost seemed like her passing was giving me permission to leave teaching. But I hadn't come to that conclusion yet. At the time of her death I was still completely devoted to setting up my classroom, learning my responsibilities and getting to know my staff and students, even though I was physically and emotionally drained at the end of every day.

Already anxious that I was in over my head with this particular teaching job, I was hesitant to take time off for Sister Libby's memorial service. But my supervisor seemed understanding when I explained my connection to Sister Libby, and she encouraged me to take the time I needed. I was going to say my final goodbye to the woman who had been my spiritual director, mentor and dear friend for over a decade.

In reality, I had been saying goodbye to her slowly and painfully for six years, ever since her failing health had forced her into retirement at the Kenwood Convent in Albany. During those years I became, as Sister Libby called me, her "most faithful friend." I visited her once a month, bringing her favorite coffee and donuts from Dunkin' Donuts. I also brought fresh flowers, which I arranged before her to her great pleasure, as well as pictures of my family and stories of my teaching, prayer life and miscellaneous adventures. I found most of our visits to be quite difficult. She was no longer the vibrant, erudite woman who had agreed to be my spiritual director in 1994. She suffered a multitude of ailments, but most disturbing was her short-term memory loss. As anyone who has watched a loved one slip away knows, this is painful.

So when I learned about Sister Libby's passing, it was bittersweet news. It had been difficult to watch her suffer, and I had prayed for an end to it. But it was still a great loss. I had yet to learn how deeply the loss would affect me on several different levels.

On the day of her memorial service, I drove the few miles to Kenwood, as I had so often done in the past, but everything seemed different. I was conscious of the finality. I knew that Kenwood would be closing soon, and there would be no reason for me to go there again. Entering the beautifully manicured grounds where the stately old building was located on North Pearl Street in Albany was like entering another dimension of time. Formerly the novitiate for RSCJ's in both the U.S. and Canada, it had become a Health Care Center for elderly, infirm and ill RSCJ's, and all of the sisters in residence were in the process of a staged, gradual movement to different retirement centers.

I was disoriented during the drive, since I was accustomed to driving to Kenwood from the Albany suburb of Colonie where I lived, rather from the city of Albany where I was teaching. I was grateful that I had arranged to meet an acquaintance I knew from Abba House at the memorial service: when we spoke on the phone about Sister Libby's passing I offered to drive this woman home if she could get to Kenwood on her own. I think I made that promise to her in order to get myself there. I did not want to go.

I did not want to cry in public. Crying in the presence of others had been difficult for me for as long as I could remember. I had always been envious of friends and family members who cried in front of others. I could weep and wail with gusto when alone, but always felt as if I had a tourniquet around my chest when I became emotional in public. That day I had purposefully thrown myself into school duties with great vigor—easy, since my teaching job was profoundly consuming—and did not get in touch with my grief until I was driving to the service.

Driving through the city streets, my hands tightened on the steering wheel and the muscles in my shoulders clenched as the sadness descended over me like a heavy blanket. I felt weighted to the seat. Each movement necessary to drive took concerted effort. I turned off the highway and into the long driveway that snaked down to the main building, scoping the area for a place to park, before pulling into what appeared to be a place near the door that had been left open just for me. After parking, I stepped out of my car into the bright sunshine, walked the short distance to the door, and entered the beautiful Kenwood Convent for what I thought might be the last time. The tightening near my heart started.

I knew the way to the chapel, as I had walked it many times on my visits to Sister Libby. During the first few years she was there, I had always stopped at the receptionist so she could call upstairs to the second floor nursing unit where Sister Libby moved when she left Abba House in 2001. Each time I entered I enjoyed the walk down the long hallway, and always paused to look at the class pictures hanging there, of the St. Agnes School graduates. (St. Agnes School was combined with Kenwood Academy during the 1970's, becoming the Doane Stuart School.) I loved looking at those beautiful girls, frozen in time in their lovely youth, and imagining what their lives had been like. The floorboards always creaked comfortingly under my feet as I made my way past the large holy statues of saints and Jesus. I liked to peek into the rooms on either side of the hallway, remembering the reception the Abba House Board members had held there in 2002, when Sister Libby and Sister Mary Gen Smyth passed the reins to the Board and the new Director of the House.

But this trip down the hallway was different. I held no flowers in my arms for my friend, no coffee cups in a cardboard holder to share. I was on my way to the chapel, not the nursing unit, and I felt unprepared for what lay ahead. I did not linger by the photographs or smile at the polished wood and immaculate tassels on the Persian rugs. The creaking of the floorboards sounded ominous instead of friendly.

A woman I did not recognize greeted me at the door and handed me a program. As I entered the long chapel, I saw the casket holding Sister Libby's earthly remains at the end of the center aisle. Glancing around the room, I saw a few familiar faces I hadn't seen since I left my seven-year tenure as an Abba House Board member in 2004. But I felt immobilized by sadness, and could not bring myself to approach anyone or sit in the chairs near the casket. Instead, I walked to the wall on the right side of the chapel, and slipped into one of the individual seats, feeling its hard, straight wood under and behind me. The ornately carved sides surrounded and isolated me in my grief.

I took a deep breath and let my eyes rest on the open casket. There she was, tiny and still. Her chin jutted up and out, showing the last vestiges of the beautiful stubbornness I had loved so much; it had made her a force to be reckoned with. She could be tough, and I needed that in my spiritual direction. I remembered her stroking her chin as she pondered my outbursts, sometimes responding with gentleness, but often coming back with a "zinger" that would resonate with me for days, or even years. She would stick out that chin when she argued with Sister Mary Gen over some Abba House-hold issue or before she uttered some proclamation over the morning paper while she ate her Cheerios and read the news. Her chin was definitive, defiant, strong and purposeful, even in death.

As my gaze travelled down to her hands, I thought about how I would never again clasp them in mine while leaning in to kiss her hello or goodbye. She had stopped eating a few months before she passed, and her hands had become very thin, like the rest of her. I stared intently at her hands as the opening music for the service commenced, and we stood to sing a gathering song. Fearing that I would sob out loud, I could not open my mouth while the other men and women sang. Instead I began to cry silently. Over and over, I thought *it's ok to cry, it's ok to cry, it's ok to cry.* I did not stop the tears. Surprised and grateful for the enormous emotion washing over me, I let the tears flow.

Sister Rose Marie Quilter, a Religious of the Sacred Heart who had known Sister Libby for many years, delivered the eulogy. She told of a brilliant woman who had worked as a chemist before she entered religious life, which gave her more worldly experience than the typical novice at that time, who usually entered after high school or upon completing college. She talked about how Libby had taught science in a New York City high school as a young nun. She told about how Libby had founded Abba House of Prayer with Mary Gen at a time when the rest of the congregation was relatively cloistered, which kept the nuns in separate living conditions, apart from the rest of the world. Starting a House of Prayer was doubly impressive because it was the first venture of its kind for the RSCJ's. Since Libby also needed an income, she enrolled in nursing school when she was in her fifties, simultaneously beginning her nursing career while at the same time embracing the adventure of running a House of Prayer. And it was Sister Libby's sense of adventure and passion for education that led to her annual foray to Boston College where she studied theology. As I listened to Sister Rose Marie's eulogy, I learned things I had not known about my friend. Sister Rose Marie was articulate and thorough, breaking down only when she made her personal goodbye at the end.

After the eulogy, I realized how little I knew Sister Libby, in spite of knowing specific details about the different stages of her life. As she had declined in health, she had often spoken to me about her childhood and family life, and I knew how she spent her final years at Abba House because it had become my "home away from home" during that time as well. I knew some of her significant contributions to the ecumenical community in Albany and her deep respect for other faith traditions. I was privy to her spirituality through the prayers and music she chose during prayer services and programs she led at the House. But there was much more to her than I ever knew. During that eulogy I saw her brilliance and energy. I understood the frustration she exhibited at times, when the wisdom and sharp sensibility of her knowledge and experience gave way to occasional impatience.

After the gentle yet very powerful service, I watched the mourners file past Sister Libby to say goodbye, and was moved by their love and grief. When it was my turn to approach the casket, I wanted so badly to kiss her. I almost expected her to open her eyes and greet me with a smile, but she did not, so I touched her jacket with love instead. Even though I knew that her spirit had already left her body, I felt her presence in the chapel, as I have so often since that moment. As I write this, I feel it still.

After everyone who had expressed a desire to speak had done so, one of the sisters talked about Sister Libby's great love for Mount Saviour Monastery in Elmira, New York. I had heard from both Sister Libby and Sister Mary Gen that the idea for starting a House of Prayer grew from a suggestion Libby received while she was on retreat there in the late 1960's. At Mount Saviour she met the Benedictine author David Steindl-Rast, who encouraged Sister Libby to open a House of Prayer, probably as part of a conversation they had about her prayer life. Sister Libby was delighted when, several years later, she took Sister Mary Gen to Mount Saviour, and found that Sister Mary Gen was equally captivated by the experience. Early in their ministry, the Sisters began a practice of making annual retreats at the monastery, where they prayed about and planned their spiritual programs for the upcoming year. I had heard them speak of Mount Saviour so often that I felt like I had been there long before I made the actual trip myself.

As a fitting final tribute to a woman who had a deep love and appreciation for both spiritual music and the simple yet profound life at Mount Saviour, a recording of Compline, the monks' evening prayer, played in the chapel. I closed my eyes and imagined the monks' faces while I remembered how Sister Libby had spoken of each of them with love and respect.

****

After the service, I found Sister Rose Marie Quilter, and told her that Sister Libby had been my spiritual director. I explained how I had visited Sister Libby often after she came to Kenwood. When I mentioned that she died on my birthday and that I was working as a teacher largely due to her encouragement, Sister Rose Marie took my hands, looked at me with love and said, "You truly were her spiritual daughter."

Have you ever experienced a deep knowing in your spirit when someone says something that touches a profound truth in you? That is what I felt at that moment. I realized the connection Sister Libby and I had was permanent, life changing and wonderful. Her wisdom and strength would continue to help me immensely during the months following her funeral when my life would take dramatic turns, both professionally, and through my return to my lifelong love of writing, as I began this book.

I have met many people through the years who have their own story to tell about Sister Libby: this is mine.

ABBA HOUSE THROUGH THE YEARS

RSCJ Origins

To everything there is a season, a time for every purpose under heaven. Ecclesiastes 3:1

While both Sister Elizabeth (Libby) Hoye and Sister Mary Gen Smyth worked tirelessly at Abba House for thirty years, Sister Libby was the visionary who initiated Abba House. As a Religious Sister of the Sacred Heart in the late 1960's, Sister Libby taught science at several schools in Connecticut and New York City. She found the busy professional life of being a teacher took up most of her time, even as she yearned a life centered in prayer and reflection, with the ultimate goal of combining prayer and active ministry.

> She [Sister Libby] had always cherished the community prayer life of her congregation, but now that seemed to be dissipating as she and her fellow sisters found they had become so busy in their work and ministry that they barely had time to pray.
>
> Excerpt from 11/7/91 Evangelist article,
> "Abba House of Prayer marks its 20th"

By 1960, the work of the Religious of the Sacred Heart as educators was expanding. Reverend Mother deValon, Superior General of the Society in 1960, wrote at that time:

> In many parts of the world arms are reaching out to us, begging for the benefit of the strong education more necessary than ever now that, little by little, faith is wavering and the sense of God is being lost. We answer these calls to the utmost of our possibilities . . . Almost everywhere our schools, colleges and training colleges are so crowded that we have to stretch the walls and put up new buildings. In these houses, which we must modernize to meet today's needs, activity is increasing and the work of our religious becomes more and more intense.
>
> The Society of the Sacred Heart: History of a Spirit,
> Margaret Williams, RSCJ, p. 263

Work of the RSCJ community was increasing prior to the Second Vatican Council, the twenty-first ecumenical council of the Roman Catholic Church that led to sweeping modernization through many aspects of the worldwide church. However, the structured prayer life of the congregation remained consistent and fostered a deep interior life of prayer and contemplation. An annual eight-day retreat focusing on the Spiritual Exercises of St. Ignatius, spiritual reading during mealtimes and rules of silence during many parts of the day supported a sense of unity within the community.

> The rhythm of personal prayer—length of time, hour of day, even place—was set by rule and settled by custom. This, the most precious of the day's occupations, was secure. The rule of silence protected recollection, the rule of cloister protected the way of life. The individual had no responsibility regarding these observances, but she was wholly responsible for the use made of this large liberty to be in the presence of God.
>
> The Society of the Sacred Heart: History of a Spirit,
> Margaret Williams, RSC, p. 325

The years following the Second Vatican Council were a time of transition for all religious orders, but the Religious of the Sacred Heart went through profound changes in their move from a cloistered to a non-cloistered congregation. Sr. Francis Gimber, RSCJ summarized some of the most significant changes in a talk she gave to the RSCJ associates in 2005. To her, the most important difference was a shift from uniformity within the community, which was viewed as a sign of fidelity to one's vocation, to a lessening of uniformity in deference to "the value of openness, responsiveness to the needs of the world, adaptation to the local culture and to the needs of individual religious." Some of the more concrete changes follow:

Before	After
specific times of day and length of time for personal prayer	individual choice of time and length of prayer
obedience to the slightest sign of the superior's will	dialog as a way of discovering the will of God
strict cloister with individual exceptions	regulation of going out according to personal and family relationships and apostolate
dependence in asking item by item for what was needed	a personal budget to be managed as well as participation in the community budget preparation

The shift from the traditional clothing/religious habit of the RSCJ, which had remained consistent for over 100 years, was not mandated by the administration, but most of the members opted for it, representing another significant change.

Sister Rose Marie Quilter remembers this transition, and the shift from silence to conversation as one of the significant changes. Prior to the Second Vatican Council, there was no conversation during mealtimes. Instead, one of the sisters would read aloud from spiritual classics or contemporary literature while the others ate. Silence was the rule during the day and after evening meals with exceptions made for short periods of recreation and any communication that involved ministry. Changes after the Council included the introduction of conversation into daily life and a breakdown of the former traditional prayer structures. The Society of the Sacred Heart, known for its contemplative, prayerful tradition, was founded by Mother

Madeleine Sophie Barat, who was adamant about the need for members to maintain an "interior spirit" of deep prayer. Structured times for the traditional periods of prayer such as daily meditation, Eucharistic adoration and the Spiritual Exercises of St. Ignatius were part of daily life in the Society prior to the Second Vatican Council. But after Vatican II, it was the individual's responsibility to seek her own rhythm of prayer. The loss of structured prayer times and the major lifestyle changes that came with them, presented difficulties for many of the sisters, and, over time, many left the Congregation. Although the reasons for these departures were complex, destabilization in spiritual practices was a contributing factor.

When Sister Libby was teaching in New York City during those transition years of the late 1960's, Sister Margaret Mary Coakley was the New York Provincial, a major superior of the congregation exercising general supervision over the New York province. On one of Sister Margaret's visits to the City, she suggested that Sister Libby visit Mount Saviour Benedictine Monastery in Elmira, New York for her private retreat; it was on this retreat that Sister Libby spoke with Brother David Steindl-Rast, a Benedictine monk who was active in the House of Prayer movement at that time. He suggested that Sister Libby open a House of Prayer, a place where religious and lay people could visit and refresh themselves by resting in God's presence, emerging renewed and ready to resume their active lives.

After Brother David planted the seed that would grow into Abba House, Sister Libby returned to New York City to fulfill her teaching obligation at a school in Harlem. Several months later she visited two of the first "model" houses of prayer—Kresge and Visitation—and along the way received valuable instruction from Sister Ann Chester, a leader in the House of Prayer movement. Sister Libby then petitioned her congregation for permission to open a new House of Prayer by submitting proposals she had written for the venture. The Congregation approved her letter-writing campaign to the convents of the Sacred Heart throughout the United States in search for like-minded sisters to join her in starting the house. Meanwhile, Sister Mary Gen Smyth was living in California, experiencing a similar desire to live a deeper prayer life. She and Sister Libby had been novices together at Kenwood Convent during the 1950's, so they had some shared experiences. Sister Mary Gen responded to the canvas letter, stating that she was interested in starting a House of Prayer.

A few friends of the sisters still remember those times. Mary Skinner, who first met Sister Libby at Mount Saviour Monastery in 1969, had traveled to the monastery without making prior reservations, and no one was available to greet her. Sister Libby was on retreat at that time and saw Mary's predicament, so she invited Mary into the house where she was staying and fed her breakfast. They became friends. On another occasion the two met at Mount Saviour, and Sister Libby needed a ride back to Kenwood, where she was to begin her ministry in the House of Prayer. Mary gave Sister Libby a ride to Kenwood, carrying her suitcases over the threshold of her new home. They remained in touch through the years, connecting during their summers at Boston College and when Mary traveled to Albany to lead a few programs at Abba House. She was a great admirer of Sister Libby and her ability to keep Abba House operative for so many years.

Kenwood Beginnings

In July of 1971, the sisters opened their House of Prayer in the former novitiate area at Kenwood, where novices had stayed prior to taking their vows. The area, located in the West Wing of Kenwood, had been renovated particularly for their use. Joining them were RSCJ Sisters Rose Marie Quilter, Mabel Dorsey and Mary Parkinson, and later Theresa (Terri) Bronner and Ines Giraldo. From the start, they intended to be an inter-congregational group, welcoming sisters from many different orders. The second

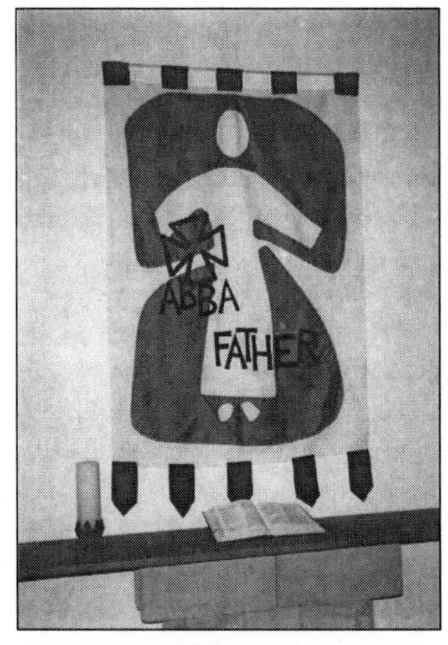

Banner from Abba House, circa 1971

year of their operation that intention became reality when Sister Augusta Power, a Sister of Saint Martha from Nova Scotia, joined them and stayed with the community for two years. All of the sisters worked part-time outside the house to earn an income.

Inside the house, the sisters maintained an atmosphere of peace and stillness conducive to prayer, reflection, study, reading or rest. Their model of living with a deeply prayerful spirit was intended to support guests in their own prayer. Twice a day the sisters gathered for group prayer, where guests were welcome to join them. Each guest had his or her own private room as well.

The members chose the name "Abba" which is the Hebrew word for "Daddy" or "Papa" because they believed the word was a prayer in itself—the prayer of the Holy Spirit in Jesus to the Father. They also knew "Abba" was a reflection of the close personal relationship Jesus had with his Father God. Jesus prayed to God using the intimate name of "Abba" and taught his disciples to do the same. The prayerful, quiet atmosphere of the Abba Community fostered silent prayer that allowed individuals to know God intimately. The deep prayer of the community helped guests connect with the great love that is always found in God's presence.

> Prayer is not an exchange of thoughts: God has no need of our thoughts, he asks for our presence. Prayer is a meeting of two loves that seek each other. Reverend Mother Sabine de Valon,
>
> The Society of the Sacred Heart: History of a Spirit,
> Margaret Williams, RSCJ, p. 291

Father Kenneth Doyle, the Kenwood chaplain at that time, celebrated the Community's first liturgy. The sisters invited many other priests to come to Abba Community to say Mass. John Sullivan, MS (Missionaries of Our Lady of LaSalette) remembered: "Abba House was an oasis of prayer for me as a young priest. That included time for personal prayer as well as the opportunity to celebrate Mass with them even when they were still living in their convent before they moved to Abba House."

Listening—more finely described as "deep listening"—was a recurrent theme in the ministry of the Abba Community. Guests who visited, whether for short periods or overnight, experienced it firsthand through its core members as well as through the rich and varied prayer activities that were offered. The founding community of five signed a document located in the Abba House archives dated November 1971 titled "ABBA COMMUNITY, Convent of the Sacred Heart, Albany, New York" from which the following is excerpted.

> The most basic intuition in the Judeo-Christian tradition, from its very beginning, is that God speaks, and because God speaks, everything can speak to us, and we can listen. This insight of Brother David Steindl-Rast, Benedictine Monk of Mount Saviour Monastery, seems to capture the spirit of our first months together as "Abba Community." We want to share our beginnings with you now in these few words, and hope that the time will come when we can speak and listen to you in person.
>
> From July until November, our primary task has been quite simply to begin our life of prayer together. Our mornings are free for prayer in private; we meet also for about an hour of shared prayer over scripture. Mid-day is occupied with work of various kinds. We take turns at cooking supper, and value the evening together as a natural time for sharing, concluded with a second hour of prayer in common. This simple rhythm of prayer, work and sharing has already been enriched by a very brief visit from Mother Camacho [RSCJ Superior General], who spoke to us of the Society's desire for prayer; by a beautiful liturgy on the theme of "Abba" in scripture, celebrated by Reverend James Cronen, O.S.B. and by the presence of Brother David, who spent two days with us in October, during which he also gave talks to the Kenwood communities, and to a varied evening audience at a public lecture here.
>
> Perhaps we could leave you with another word from Brother David: "Need less and less; thank more and more." It is because our prayer has led us in the direction

> of thankfulness to the Father through the Son, in the Holy Spirit, that we cry: 'Abba, Father!'
>
> We wish now to thank all who have steadily encouraged us in this quiet beginning.

The Community opened for guests in February of 1972 at their Kenwood location. Their self-contained apartment in Kenwood on the West Wing, second floor, included a chapel, living room, dining room, kitchen, private rooms for each of the five founding members and seven guest rooms. A flyer described their apostolate as giving special witness to the value of prayer and helping to provide a suitable place and atmosphere where others could come to pray. The Community asked for a donation of $5 per day from visiting guests to meet the expenses of operating the House.

Sister Mary Gen remembered that four sisters from a different order came to visit the early Abba Community and were impressed by its operation. They asked the sisters who were running the House of Prayer to teach them how they lived in community.

Theresa (Terri) Bronner was a member of the Abba Community during the early years. She said that the facilities at Kenwood weren't exactly conducive to what they were trying to do, since they occupied a section of the former novitiate area, but the location served to get the house "off the ground." She remembers it as a real experiment, since members of the Society were just beginning to expand into parish ministries. According to Terri, the early years were a period of testing, to see if it would be successful, but "it tested out pretty well, pretty quickly." Terri added "The House of Prayer was really groundbreaking at that time. It seemed to fill a need—people from all walks of life came to it. At that time, there weren't many places where people could go to pray in community. It was a tenuous start, but the Sisters were passionate and committed."

At the close of the first year, one of the five members of the Abba Community, Sister Rose Marie Quilter, RSCJ, wrote a reflection called "Houses of Prayer: Crossroads" which included the following excerpts. The theme of the piece was "convergence and integration," and Sister Rose Marie wrote it after she read an article by Sister Ann Chester about the House of Prayer Movement.

> I would like to describe something of this experience of convergence and integration as it is taking place in one small House of Prayer, Abba Community, which is just celebrating its first year of existence.
>
> Since last February, guests have converged on our home in search of an atmosphere of silence; time and space for solitude and reflection; sharing in prayer, conversation and Eucharist. About 140 sisters and laywomen have come, their stays ranging from a day to a month or more. More than 100 others have come for brief visits—an afternoon of prayer or an evening liturgy and supper. Forty priests have celebrated the Eucharist in our living room or chapel; many of them return regularly. Housewives, students, teachers, missionaries, seminarians, workers in hospitals and the inner city, men and women engaged in pastoral ministry—they come, and they share, and they pray alone or together, and around the hearthfire of the Eucharist and the meal that follows it.
>
> But to say this is still to describe the surface of a House of Prayer experience. The movement towards integration reaches the depths, but insofar as it occurs, it is part of the hidden and awesome action of the Spirit, so no words can do it justice. However, we may attempt to reflect on this growth towards wholeness as it happens in a House of Prayer. Integration begins with individuals. That is, when our guests and we live in such an atmosphere, we have an opportunity to open ourselves to the Word of God, because we have that rarest of luxuries—an opportunity to listen. Integration happens also within the sharing community. It does not happen smoothly, without anguish. This growth toward wholeness seems to participate in the rhythms characteristic of all living things- there is a time when the seed sleeps underground, and the moment

when it bursts through the hard soil, and the days when it stretches toward the sunlight or drinks in the rain.

A true asceticism of listening is imposed on a small community whose members individually want nothing more intensely than to hear the Word of God and keep it. The Holy Spirit leads them to the realization that if they wish to hear the Word of God, they must listen hard to each other, and become sensitive to the way in which the Word speaks to the others, and to all the group as a whole. An awesome realization begins to dawn: the supposition on which shared prayer is founded is that Jesus is in the midst of us when we pray, if we are gathered together in His Name—and so the challenge grows: to gather together truly in His Name, to listen when He speaks in our midst, and the keep His Word, "day by day" as the song from *Godspell* puts it.

Move to Western Avenue: "Nuns as Neighbors"

Jesus said to them, "The harvest truly is great, but the laborers are few. Therefore pray the Lord of the harvest to send out laborers into his harvest."

Luke 10:2

Abba House at 647 Western Avenue, 1973

In early 1973, after two years at Kenwood, the Abba Community went in search of a home of its own apart from Kenwood for a variety of reasons, including the desire to be among the lay community it was supporting. After searching for property in Albany for several months, the small Community moved from Kenwood to its new home on Western Avenue. Two priests in the Albany diocese who often visited the Abba Community at Kenwood for prayer, liturgy and fellowship assisted with the search and the move. Father John J. (J.J.) Rooney scanned real estate listings in the capital district, envisioning the Community in a more homelike atmosphere, where he hoped to someday bring young people from the Diocesan Search program for retreats. The Sisters also had assistance from Father Paul Roman, whom they had met in the early 1970's when Father Roman was a newly ordained priest at St. James parish on Delaware Avenue. Sister Libby liked to recall how they met at St. James church, where the four Abba House founding sisters often attended daily Mass. One day Father Roman approached them after Mass and asked them, "So, where are you girls from?" That was the beginning of a long and meaningful friendship, which included Father Roman's role as Sister Libby's confessor and spiritual director.

When the Sisters began searching for a new home for Abba House, they looked for a building in the city for their House of Prayer. Father Roman sometimes drove them around to view the houses since he knew his way around the city, having grown up on Sheridan Avenue in Albany. After Father Rooney found the building at 647 Western Avenue, which was constructed in 1912, Father Roman's mother helped the sisters set up their kitchen by supplying them with a dining room table, and some dishes and pans from spare kitchen supplies in her basement. When they moved into the house, Father Roman was a frequent guest and Mass celebrant for many years. As is often the case with Diocesan priests, he moved relatively often from parish to parish, but noted that his transfers did not dampen his friendship with the Abba Community: "Wherever I was, they found me," he was fond of saying. Sister Libby and Sister Mary Gen would visit him wherever he was stationed and invite him to the House for supper, to say a Mass, or to lead a program.

"They were pioneers."
Father Paul Roman

Sister Libby and Sister Mary Gen settled solidly into their Western Avenue home, where they were "good neighbors" according to Carmela Richards, who lived next door. She recalls that they were both friendly and outgoing. Everyone in the neighborhood knew them, especially after they initiated annual picnics in the late 1980's. She shared some sweet memories of her interactions with them through the years:

- How the Sisters borrowed the family dog for an activity they were having in the yard with the young people of the Search program in the 1970's;
- How they would wave to each other from the kitchens of their respective houses whenever they looked out and saw each other;
- How they visited her with gifts when she had moved away for a time and they learned she had given birth to her daughter;
- How they joked about putting signs up to direct the birds and squirrels to each other's yards, since the Sisters fed the birds and Carmela fed the squirrels.

Another friend from the neighborhood who has pleasant memories of the Sisters and the House is Pat Doyle. She recalls knocking on their door one day in the fall of 1980 after she had moved back to Albany during a transition period. Having read an article about the House in the *Evangelist*, the Albany Roman Catholic Diocesan newspaper, she was curious, although admittedly a bit apprehensive since she had "little experience praying in small groups." She was relieved when she found that the Sisters were out doing a radio interview the day she knocked on the door, so she didn't feel obligated to join in prayer on her first visit. Instead, she met a friend of the House who was folding flyers and stuffing envelopes for a mailing, so she stayed and helped while they listened to the Sisters on the radio. According to Pat, "that day typified the low-key, friendly, welcoming atmosphere of Abba House." Through the years she participated in programs, was invited to join the Board of Directors, traveled to Mount Saviour for a retreat with the Sisters, led a program at the House and was able to use the lessons learned there to cope with a "wonderful but challenging" job in the health care field. She recalls "I treasure the memories from my years at Abba House and appreciate the gentle guidance I received from Sister Libby and Sister Mary Gen."

Sister Libby and Sister Mary Gen continued to work outside the House to bring in wages that they gave to their order, which in turn paid them a modest stipend. Those jobs brought them into the community in practical ways. At first, Sister Mary Gen worked as a bookkeeper at Kenwood, then in a law firm, where she met a young lawyer—Bartley J. Costello (BJ)—and forged a friendship and business relationship that lasted for the thirty-year span of the House, and beyond. Sister Mary Gen also worked for several years as a secretary at St. Catherine of Siena School, where her supervisor was the school's principal, Joseph McTighe, who would later become the first president of the Abba House Board of Directors. Sister Libby worked nights and weekends at the Kenwood Infirmary as a nurse after earning her nursing degree at Maria College.

Both Sisters worked until 1980, when they stopped work outside Abba House because the activity at the House became fuller, bringing in more income. The House derived most of its modest annual income (approximately $35-40,000) from a combination of program fees, fundraising and board fees for long-term boarders and retreatants. Abba House was always financially independent of the Albany Roman Catholic Diocese.

As they had been at Kenwood before they moved to Western Avenue, the House continued to be intercongregational, with Anglican sisters Mary Clare Smith, OSA (Order of St. Anne) and Augusta Powers, CSM (Companion of the Sacred Mission) in residence, along with Sister Ines Geraldo, RSCJ and Sister Kathleen Ann Humphrey, SNJM (Sisters of the Holy Names of Jesus and Mary) joining them at various times. The Abba Community welcomed individuals and groups of RSCJ from Kenwood on a regular basis, as well as many priests, students, and laypersons.

Some of the early work of the House included accommodating the Search program for young people of the Albany diocese, hosting Diocesan programs and committee meetings, offering Bible study classes, traveling to parish halls or homes to pray with others as requested, praying in community for two hours each day and offering liturgies for guests and neighbors several times each week.

> *"It took a tremendous amount of courage for them to come out of the convent in the 1970's."*
>
> *B.J. Costello*

There were challenges along the way, of course, but most of them did not make it into the archives, though they were alluded to by some of the individuals interviewed for this writing. The challenges must have been met with prayer, along with a good dose of that "dogged determination" that Sister Ann Chester described in Sister Libby. Sister Rose Marie Quilter estimates that three out of four RSCJ's were against the congregation investing anything in this new venture at the beginning, although the formal leadership showed support by providing space for the community at Kenwood. Sister Jean Ford, who was the Provincial of the Washington Province and on the General Council at the time Abba House started, estimated the percentage of RSCJ's opposed to the idea was even higher: about 90 percent. According to Sister Jean, "They already had retreats and prayer was integral to their lives. This House of Prayer was to be apart from the community: it was very different." The congregation had just recently emerged from cloister in 1967, which resulted in significant shifts in their prayer styles and even their places of residence, as many moved out into individual parish communities. Now this idea came. Another of the early members of the community, Sister Mary Parkinson, interviewed at Teresian House in Albany, where she lived in retirement in 2009, remembered the challenges of the early years: "when you start something, you don't always get 100 percent support, although you need it. It's hard to keep on going without that, but they did, and did a good job, too!"

We live at a crossroads. As the circle of our guests widens, putting us in touch with many needs, we know that we, least of all, can afford to be turned in on ourselves. Convergence and integration send us out to speak the Word of God we have heard in silence, to feed those who hunger for the bread of life.

"Houses of Prayer: Crossroads" RM Quilter

My House—Introduction to a "Prayer Life" and Abba House

In 1994 I became one of several thousand people whose lives intersected with Abba House of Prayer. My arrival at the House resulted from a chain of events that began with some lifestyle changes I made in my early thirties. I started making different choices that led me to a new way of living and the beginning of an exciting spiritual journey that stretched me nearly to breaking, but also provided amazing, rich experiences.

A significant step of that spiritual journey began when I started bringing a new energy and interest to my Roman Catholic faith tradition, and particularly to the faith community I was involved with at the time: Our Lady of Mercy Parish (OLM) in Colonie, New York. My husband brought me to OLM when we married in 1989. My son by my first marriage, whom my husband later adopted, was enrolled in a Catholic school in another local parish. My second son had been born in 1992, and the four of us were happily enjoying our family life, including attending weekly Mass at OLM. My husband knew many people in the parish, having been a member there for about 30 years when he was raising his older children from his first marriage. I, however, felt disconnected and out of place. I realized that I had to make a service commitment to the church in order to truly become a part of it. I had to give something of myself in order to receive the gift of community I desired.

One week, I saw a notice in the bulletin that interested me: the parish needed Children's Liturgy of the Word leaders. It sounded manageable—a commitment of once every few weeks during the Sunday10:30 am Mass, which we attended every week. So I made the call to find out exactly what being a leader entailed, embarking on my first venture into catechesis, an area of my life that has gifted me enormously through the years with spiritual growth, amazing friends, and most importantly, the opportunity to speak about my faith. When I made that first commitment, I was promised "helps" in the form of resources to prepare for my role as a leader of Children's Liturgy of the Word. I would be responsible for "breaking open" the Sunday readings with the young people who left the congregation for their own Liturgy of the Word during the Mass. I was excited.

The wonderful women who organized Children's Liturgy at our church arranged periodic faith-sharing evenings so the catechists could connect in a prayerful environment that also offered community. I remember my first evening with them. I felt somewhat out of place—this "spiritual stuff" was new and foreign to me, and I only knew the names of a few of the people at the gathering. But as I looked around the large circle of chairs where all these women and a few men sat, I saw friendly faces that were open and welcoming. Even though I felt uncomfortable reading the prayers and singing, I did my best to act as if I knew what I was doing—a hallmark of my spiritual experiences that followed in the years ahead. I was clueless about the adventure that awaited me, which was probably a good thing: I have always enjoyed surprises, and God has never disappointed me!

That first evening, one of the women described a dryness she was experiencing in her prayer life. She said she was sitting on a swing in a playground where she had brought her children, and she was feeling empty and rather sad. She asked God "Is there something wrong with my prayer life?" Other women in the group were quick to comfort and reassure her, mentioning that she had just that year given birth to her fifth child. Being a mother to five young children can be overwhelming and consuming, and she was preparing to return to work. I saw a beautiful demonstration of community in the way she was loved and supported that evening,

I also got stuck on her question: "is there something wrong with my ***prayer life***?" That statement resonated deeply in my spirit: I knew that it meant something pivotal to me personally.

As I pondered it I realized: I did not HAVE a ***prayer life!*** What a realization that was!

Walking out to the parking lot after the gathering, I connected in conversation with another woman who was to become my Children's Liturgy partner and friend in the near future.

"It's Amy, right? I'm Anne"

"Hi Anne. Wasn't that amazing?"

"That's exactly what I was thinking! I've never experienced anything like that," I said. It felt good to admit that out loud.

"I'm really excited about this, but I'm new at it," Amy said.

"I am too! Maybe we can help each other," I said. "It would be great to have a partner in Children's Liturgy."

And so our friendship and catechetical partnership was born. As we worked together on the Sundays we led the Children's Liturgy, Amy and I developed a comfortable way of building on each other's comments to the children, which was my first experience with team teaching. She is a beautiful woman with a deep connection to God, and I have learned much from her through the years.

That night when I got in my car my head was swimming with all the events of the evening: the prayers, music and fellowship. What an incredibly exciting time it was and how blessed I felt! And that new term—***prayer life***—seemed to ripple through me. I resolved to be on the lookout for opportunities to grow one of those for myself!

****

One of the opportunities our church offered its catechists was attendance at Spring Enrichment, an annual four-day conference organized by the Albany diocese. Held at the local College of Saint Rose, the conference is always an incredible event with an abundance of rich spiritual delicacies I have come to savor. Two-hour classes are offered on many different topics leading to various levels of catechetical certification. I look forward to the event each year because there is often something on the menu for me. Many of the classes have led to new avenues of spiritual experience and growth in my life.

One of the classes offered at Spring Enrichment in 1994 was an introduction to Centering Prayer. As it was defined in the class, and as I have come to know it during the years I have practiced it, Centering Prayer is Christ-centered meditation. The brief description of the class that called it "heart-centered meditation" appealed to me. Venturing into the realm of prayer and meditation as I began to grow a ***prayer life*** of my own, I signed up for the class. After a brief introduction, the instructor said we would try this type of prayer together in the class. She led us through a brief guided meditation and we fell into silence.

She told us to inhale peace and exhale any negativity; to inhale the Holy Spirit and exhale frustration, angst, and any anger we were feeling. She encouraged us to follow the in breath through our nostrils, where it felt cool and light, down the throat, expanding the chest and belly. I felt as if I were sinking into my core, where I found the Divine Spark after whose image and likeness I am made. I experienced a deep peace and connection to God in those few moments, something that felt like bliss. It left me hungry for more. I suspect that I was given something like a spiritual appetizer, awakening a part of me that seemed to have been dormant for years.

At the end of the two-hour class, the instructor suggested that if the workshop had been a positive prayer experience and we wished to continue on this path, we should try to find a spiritual director. She said spiritual direction was available through several local retreat houses and in some parishes. I promised myself I would pursue this.

Within a month or so, I opened the phone book and looked in the yellow pages under "prayer." I found what looked like a promising entry: Abba House of Prayer on Western Avenue in Albany, New York. I dialed the number and spoke with the woman who answered, Sister Libby Hoye. After describing the experience I had with Centering Prayer at Spring Enrichment, I asked if there were someone there who might be able to provide spiritual direction. Sister Libby said, "I think I can do that!" and we made an appointment.

Abba House was set up on a hill a bit back on Western Avenue, a busy main street in Albany. It looked like a residence and had a small, unassuming sign in front. (I later heard it described it as "the best kept secret in the city.") I drove there for the first of many times on a summer afternoon in July. After pulling into the driveway off a side street, I mounted a few steps to the door of the screened porch. When I rang the bell, an energetic woman with sparkling eyes, silver curls and a ready smile greeted me at the door: Sister Mary Gen Smyth, a dynamic, effervescent woman who had founded the house with Sister Libby in the 1970's. After we introduced ourselves, she asked if I was there to see Libby and showed me into one of their quiet sitting rooms. A few minutes later, Sister Libby walked in and introduced herself.

Sister Libby was small and somewhat on the round side. She walked carefully, leaning on the furniture as she passed. She had short, straight, brown hair, and wore glasses with bright eyes shining behind them. She had a sweet smile. I could not guess her age at first, but I now know that she was in her seventies. At that point she struck me as rather ageless. She spoke slowly and deliberately, but was at the same time friendly and welcoming. I thought she seemed wise and rather all-knowing.

Sister Libby asked me what I wanted, and I told her I wanted to learn how to pray and develop my spiritual life. She offered to provide suggestions in that area, and her first was that I read some sacred Scripture daily, to complement my new practice of daily Centering Prayer. She suggested we meet regularly to discuss my progress. We agreed I would call and make appointments for our meetings, and so I began my forays to Abba House.

I probably did not offer a financial donation at that time, which is what led to the mini-lecture I received from her the next time I visited. As I said, I was clueless about this new venture. Who knows what I was thinking? In a way, entering Abba House was like going to a foreign country. I recall wondering, "what exactly *IS* a House of Prayer?" Remember, I did not have a ***prayer life***. What did they do all day? Maybe I thought their financial needs were met by their order, like the sisters who had taught me in Catholic school as a child. In any case, at my second appointment a few weeks later, Sister Libby set me straight, explaining that she and Sister Mary Gen needed to put food on the table. Mortified, I immediately whipped out my checkbook and asked what a reasonable donation would be. I never forgot again.

It wasn't long after I started going to Abba House that I reached a crisis point in my emotional life, and my therapist encouraged me to take some time by myself. She asked if there were anywhere I could go to get away from my home, where life was becoming increasingly chaotic and difficult. My older son, who was eleven at the time, had begun to change dramatically with the onset of puberty. He was becoming rebellious, defiant, moody, and sometimes very sad. That may sound like pretty standard teenage behavior, but I knew there was more there. My wonderful husband had already raised five children to adulthood during his first marriage and had bravely embarked on a new family with me at a time in his life when most men were settling into grandparenting. He was not dealing well with the intense mood swings of the boy he had adopted. Our younger son was a joy, but even he, at the age of two, was starting to be affected by the disruption in our home. At the same time, I was in frequent pain from what was eventually diagnosed as endometriosis, a chronic health condition caused by excessive uterine tissue growth in the abdominal cavity, which caused intense pain approximately three out of four weeks each month. I was exhausted. I desperately wanted to do the right things—to love my family and grow in my relationship with God—but I was physically and emotionally depleted.

As I sat in my therapist's office and pondered where I might go to "get away from it all," I remembered the sisters at Abba House of Prayer. During one of my visits, Sister Mary Gen had taken me on a tour of their house. They had several guest rooms where people could stay for individual retreats. The cost was reasonable and included meals with the sisters. From my seat on the couch in my therapist's office, I looked out the window and into a beautiful blue sky. As I spoke about going to Abba House, a single large bird came into view and soared gracefully within the rectangle of sky inside the windowpane. He seemed to beckon me to follow. I felt a conviction in my soul: going to Abba House was the right thing to do.

I left that appointment feeling a little lighter, but still needing comfort. I happened to be near one of my favorite bakeries, Bella Napoli in Latham, New York, so I stopped and picked up some sweet treats for my guys and me. While I sat in my van and enjoyed a pastry with a cup of coffee, I saw a small flock of sparrows eating crumbs on the ground near the car. They were so close I could look into their eyes. As I gazed at their downy feathers and sweet little bodies, I imagined one of them cupped in my hands. I could feel the softness of its wings and the fragile bones underneath. I even felt its tiny heart beating against my palm. I cried tears of joy and gratitude, not understanding at first why, but then realizing: I was like this little bird in God's hands, and he loved and cared for me. He was greatly pleased with my own heart beating in love and the desire to know Him better. What a beautiful and profoundly moving experience to have —in the parking lot of an Italian bakery while eating delicious pastry!

ABBA HOUSE—THE FOUNDRESSES

Sister Mary Gen Smyth and Sister Libby Hoye, Abba House Chapel, circa 1990

Sister Libby Hoye

Sister Libby was born Elizabeth Genevieve Hoye on December 7, 1920 in New Bedford, Massachusetts. Her parents were Laura Agnes Powers Hoye and Frederick William Hoye, DDS. Libby and her younger sister, Kathryn Bertilde Hoye (Pichette), grew up in New Bedford, where their father was a dentist who had an office in their home. In 1942, Libby graduated magna cum laude with a Bachelor of Arts degree in Chemistry from Wheaton College in Norton, Massachusetts. Her father died relatively young, when Libby was in her twenties, and her sister was still in college. Libby worked as a research chemist, first with General Electric and then with Monsanto in Everett, Massachusetts.

In 1950, at the age of 30, Sister Libby entered the Society of the Sacred Heart. She had lived independently for several years before deciding to become a nun. Her niece Ann tells a story about Libby that she heard from her grandmother, Libby's mother, who lived with Ann and her family for many years. While Libby was working as a research chemist at Monsanto, she was involved in a laboratory accident that temporarily blinded her. According to Libby's mother, while hospitalized waiting for the bandages to be removed and to learn out whether she would regain her sight, Libby promised God that if she were to recover her vision she would become a nun. When her bandages were removed, she could see normally. Several years later, she entered religious life. When she spoke to Sister Mary Gen about this time in her life, Sister Libby did not speak of a promise to God, but did remark that her doctor at the time helped her to heal by praying for her.

The years Sister Libby spent in the Society of the Sacred Heart before 1971, the year she started Abba House, were busy and productive. She took her final vows in the Society in Rome during July of 1958. She earned two Master's degrees, one in education, and one in chemistry. In the 1960's she taught chemistry, biology and religion in high schools operated by the Society in Connecticut, Michigan and New York City. An excerpt from the eulogy for Sister Libby, provided by Sister Rose Marie Quilter follows.

> Intellectually gifted, firmly grounded in sacred scripture and prayer, a person of common sense and humor, Libby was a wonderful teacher. She and her students at 91st Street in New York were able, by the early 1960's, to attend lectures given by theologians of many denominations, as well as bishops on their way to and from Vatican Council II. It was at this time that Libby's lifelong interest in ecumenism took shape. In addition, she broadened her

> horizons and those of her students, by taking them to visit temples, synagogues and mosques. The edifice of Libby's life was progressing along interesting lines.

Sister Judy Brown, who at the time of my interview lived at the renovated Abba House in a community of retired Sisters of the Sacred Heart, recounted a story she heard Sister Libby tell about her teaching in a Harlem middle school where her students were "not too familiar with the finer points of social grace." She promised to take the girls to a fine restaurant if they could learn to behave more appropriately. After working on their behavior for some time in the classroom, she took the girls to the restaurant and reported on their successful outing: a waitress even commented on how well behaved the students were!

Sister Libby described her life in the 1960's.

> Then came the era of Vatican II. During the next 10 or 15 years much in religious life changed and storms blew away many formerly stable elements, including my habit and veil. Those were amazing years and one constantly adapted to new lifestyles and challenges. However, I had grown up by the Atlantic shore and I knew about the stability of rocks and bulkheads in storms. It was then that I clung to God as Rock, and studied the many Scripture passages, which name him as such.
>
> RSCJ newsletter 1989 "Why the Sisterhood"
> by Libby Hoye, RSCJ

Despite the many changes in daily life the RSCJ sisters were experiencing they worked very hard. They endured long days as schoolteachers, where their non-teaching periods were frequently filled with supervision duties for non-academic classes. In the evenings, it was not unusual for these same teachers to supervise dormitories where boarding students lived during the school year. Yet somehow, in the midst of all their work, they found time for classroom preparation. These were the same women who had chosen the Religious of the Sacred Heart as a result of their deep longing for a contemplative prayer life.

In some way, this series of changes and circumstances set the stage for the House of Prayer movement, and provided the impetus for Sister Libby to pursue a House of Prayer in Albany. She may have left traditional teaching in structured RSCJ settings, but she continued as an educator until the end of her life, leading adults to explore their own spirituality by way of prayer and Scripture study.

Sister Libby's full and fruitful life at Abba House did not keep her from family commitments. She maintained close connections with her sister and brother-in-law, and their family of five, who lived in Claremont, California, where she and Mary Gen visited every few years. Libby outlived her oldest niece, Marie, who died of cancer several years before Libby died. She kept a picture of Marie in her room and referred to her often. She also kept a large framed family portrait of her and her sister's family, from one of her niece's weddings. She had three nieces and one nephew, as well as eight grand nieces and two grand nephews.

As Sister Libby got closer to end of her life, she spoke more often about her childhood. I remember one of many conversations we had when I was visiting her at Kenwood.

"How are the boys, Anne?" she asked from her chair. I had finished arranging the flowers on the low bureau opposite her and we had settled down with our coffees. She was nibbling on a glazed doughnut I had brought her.

"They are doing well, Sister," I answered. "The older one is working at the market and behaving himself. I am taking the younger one to classes in Niskayuna to get his lifeguard certification."

"That's a great investment—it will serve him well as long as he keeps it up. I lifeguarded for years when I was a young woman and it provided me with steady income through college."

"Yes, I remembered your telling me that when he began to show aptitude as a swimmer, and encouraged him to get his certification as well," I said, realizing once again what a significant influence Sister Libby had on my family's life.

" I always loved to swim," Libby said, somewhat wistfully. "My father used to wake me up at dawn and take me to the sea for a swim when I was a girl in New Bedford. The water was warmer than the rest of the New England waters because we lived by a bay. I would swim behind him, parallel to the shore." She smiled and commented, "those were good times" before taking another bite of her donut.

Sister Libby continued to swim regularly for exercise at the Jewish Community Center in Albany until illness kept her from going in the late 1990's.

One of Sister Libby's last spiritual directors, Father James Cronen, OSB (Order of St. Benedict) was a member of the Benedictine community at Mount Saviour Monastery for decades. He knew Sister Libby from the late 1960's, when she first came to Mount Saviour. When interviewed for this writing, he commented that he was impressed with Sister Libby's drive and energy in opening a House of Prayer and keeping it going with Sister Mary Gen for so many years. He appreciated all of their responsibilities: finding a house, keeping it operational for thirty years, offering programs there and in the Albany community. He noted that "Sister Libby had sharp insight and the ability to get things done—some of that might have come from her science background."

Sister Mary Gen Smyth

Sister Mary Genevieve Smyth was born June 30, 1929 in St. Louis, Missouri, the oldest of three siblings. Her father, Joseph Henry Smyth, was a doctor and an Anglican priest; her mother, Lillian Adelaide West, was a teacher. Her father ministered to Native Americans in New Mexico, Arizona and California until Mary Gen was a teenager. According to Sister Mary Gen, her father had a lifelong dream of being a missionary, where he could combine his two professions of priest and doctor. He attained his goal when he went first to the Bahamas and then to Liberia as a missionary. After Mary Gen graduated from high school, she and her mother and siblings moved to Seattle, where Mary Gen worked in a public library and attended Seattle University, a Jesuit school. While in Seattle she, her mother and siblings converted to Catholicism, which upset her father considerably. Eventually he decided, when he returned from the mission field, to re-join the Order of the Holy Cross monastery in New York State, a community he had belonged to for ten years prior to marrying his wife.

While taking classes at Seattle University, Mary Gen became aware of her vocation to religious life and researched different orders. She decided on the Society of the Sacred Heart after visiting Reverend Mother Agnes Reagan in Seattle. She also visited Reverend Mother Ursula Benziger at the Mother House in Rome, Italy while on a college trip to Europe. Upon her return to the United States, she stopped in Albany and visited Reverend Mother Gertrude Bodkin and Mother Marie Louise Schroen at Kenwood. On May 31, 1951, at twenty-one years of age and only two years after her conversion to Catholicism, she entered religious life at Kenwood. After her father learned of her commitment to life as a religious, he visited her whenever he could, happy with the life and family she had chosen.

For twenty years, Sister Mary Gen worked in various capacities as an RSCJ. She first taught third and sixth grade students, then worked in several business offices as a bookkeeper. After a six month sabbatical at a Cistercian Monastery—Our Lady of the Redwoods Monastery in Whitethorn, California—she learned about the House of Prayer movement. She heard that Sister Libby was looking for RSCJ's to start a House in Albany. So, in September of 1971 she went to Albany to begin a span of thirty years at Abba House that was rich in both prayer and activity.

"Sister Mary Gen always seemed to have a twinkle in her eye."
Father Leo O'Brien

Together, Sister Libby and Sister Mary Gen were an interesting combination. To the casual observer, they would often sound as if they were disagreeing when conversing, although in actuality they were agreeing: their personalities and communication styles were quite different. They even attended Marriage Encounter, calling themselves "the odd couple." Obviously they worked well together, given the success of their thirty-year ministry.

Several people interviewed for this writing commented on their relationship. Walt Chura, a friend of the House who gave several presentations there over the years, summarized their relationship succinctly: "They were a perfect team: they were so different but they complemented each other so well." Another friend of the House, Episcopal Deacon Nancy Rosenblum, was Secretary of the Board for several years and enjoyed watching the interaction between the two sisters. She noted that when Sister Mary Gen called Sister Libby "Sister Elizabeth" she knew she was upset with her. Nancy characterized Sister Libby as "the visionary" and Sister Mary Gen as "the practical one." Justine Guernsey, who enjoyed spiritual direction with Sister Libby for a number of years, noted "they could get snappish with each other, but you always knew that they loved each other." And once when I mentioned in conversation with Sister Libby about how different they were, she responded that they "pray[ed] well together—that's all that matters."

When Sister Libby left Abba House for health reasons in 2001, Sister Mary Gen planned to leave as well. She worked with the Board members to find someone to run the House. After handing over the reins of the House to Sister Rosemary Sgroi, RSM (Sisters of Mercy), Sister Mary Gen returned to her roots by moving to Soboba Reservation in San Jacinto, California. There she worked as a secretary and sacristan for St. Joseph Mission Church, happy and active until 80+ years, with a fruitful life and a network of friends and family that she kept in touch with via e-mail, phone, and visits. In 2012 Sister Mary Gen had a stroke that left her with some paralysis, and she was moved to the Teresian House in Albany New York for community and care with other RSCJ's. On September 18, 2013, she passed away peacefully.

> *"What has kept us together is this common love of prayer," Sister Libby added. "You come to know the most beautiful part of a person in prayer; their spiritual side. You come to be more tolerant of one another, more loving."*
>
> *Excerpt from 11/7/91 Evangelist article, "Abba House of Prayer marks its 20th"*

My House

First Retreat at Abba House

If I could sum up the appeal Abba House had for me personally in one word it would be: hospitality. Never in my life had I been to a place where I felt so welcomed, loved and cared for. On each occasion I "retreated" there—which often felt like more of a retreat from battle than a spiritual retreat—I was cradled in care from the moment I entered. This was a new kind of hospitality for me, because it was love with a loose grip and gentle hand. I'm sure that level of love grew out of Sister Libby's and Sister Mary Gen's deep conviction of their purpose: to offer a place for people to come and grow in their relationship with God. I always felt privileged to be part of their spiritual community.

Each of the sisters contributed wonderful gifts and talents to Abba House. Sister Mary Gen's creativity was evident in the distinctive flavor of each of the guest rooms, where the curtains, bedspreads and bedding were carefully color-coordinated, a quality I appreciated because I enjoy sewing, knitting and other crafts. Sister Mary Gen sewed the curtains, made collages with Scripture verses and nature scenes, and framed beautiful photographs she had taken during her travels throughout the country and abroad. A few years after I began doing retreats at Abba House, the sisters asked me to join their Board of Directors, and at Christmas time, Sister Mary Gen created a calendar for the Board members. They were lovely, memorable works of art that I looked forward to receiving each year.

Sister Mary Gen sometimes seemed to be in perpetual motion, working hard doing many different tasks around the house, but always making time to be present to the guests. One of my most vivid memories of Sister Mary Gen is how she would sit down with such gusto in her chair after lunch when we gathered for afternoon prayer. With an audible exhalation, she would descend so hard that she bounced; then she would sigh and give a sweet smile to anyone who happened to be in the room. Now we were ready to pray!!

Sister Libby was businesslike in her attention to finances and fundraising. As I got to know her and the workings of the house better, I appreciated more and more her efforts in keeping the house operational. I often overheard her making phone calls in her office, which was adjacent to the guest room where I usually stayed. She put together many of the prayer services I enjoyed at the House, taught Bible studies and gave presentations on spirituality. And, of course, she did much more that I never experienced firsthand, especially in the ecumenical community in Albany.

My first spiritual retreat at Abba House, in October of 1994, is a precious memory. I was nervous about leaving my family as the situation in our home had become somewhat volatile, and I was greatly enmeshed. I had a co-dependent sense that I could somehow control everyone's tempers simply by being physically present at home. One of the blessings I received from my time at Abba House was the beginning of a realization that I did <u>not</u> control my family members or their tendencies. (Surprise!) The full revelation of that truth came slowly and gradually as my retreats over the years, first at Abba House and then at other places of prayer and renewal, grew more frequent.

I see now that the first time I entered Abba House with a suitcase was the launch of a great adventure, like a boat ride with God at the helm and me next to him. Through the years the boat has varied from a speedboat to a paddlewheel to a cruise ship, depending on life circumstances, but it has always been an awesome trip! I have the sisters of Abba House to thank for drawing me into the boat, by making the journey inviting and safe. At the House, any surprises that came were usually pleasant, and if I did not want to be a part of any exchange, I could simply retreat to my room. So I could step out into this exciting world of spiritual experience and growth whenever I felt ready, but the sisters never inundated or overwhelmed me, the way that many aspects of the rest of my life seemed to do.

Still, I do remember being anxious and not knowing what to expect when I entered the House for my first retreat. I was sure there would be rules and was afraid I would break them, not at all surprising as a lot of my life was fear-based and had been for a very long time. But Sister Mary Gen greeted me with care and kindness, showing me to my room and explaining how things were done around the House. In my room, which she said was the best guest room, Sister Mary Gen showed me how to open the windows and where to find the key to the house. She encouraged me to go for a walk to the nearby pond. She pointed out the bookcase full of spiritual resources in the hallway and the chapel where I was welcome to pray at any time. I was already familiar with the large library downstairs, and she encouraged me to borrow anything I wanted to read. She also invited me to join her and Sister Libby for afternoon prayer. Dinnertime was announced by a bell, while breakfast and lunch were "pick-up meals," meaning that I was free to help myself to anything in the fridge, closet or breadbox. I was introduced to coffee "singles" which I could use to brew individual cups whenever I wanted, and the cookie jar was always full. There was a lot to learn about the House, but as we moved from room to room, I became more relaxed; this was a safe place.

Sister Libby stopped by my room and welcomed me. Since I had already spent time with Sister Libby, I was more at ease around her. She reiterated the meal plan and Sister Mary Gen's invitation to afternoon prayer. Although I did not commit to the prayer, I was curious about how these two women— so different in temperament and demeanor—prayed together.

When Sister Libby left me to settle in, I wasn't even sure whether to close the door. Would that be rude? This was their house, after all. I was a guest. On the occasions when I had been an overnight guest in other people's houses, I usually felt compelled to be useful, or in their presence, or making conversation. This was the first time I had taken "alone time" for myself, other than an occasional few hours, such as the catechist evening of reflection when I discovered I didn't have a ***prayer life***.

****

I remember many of the details of this time because I started journaling regularly. Writing has always felt natural to me. From the time I was about twelve years old I had wanted to be a "writer." My undergraduate degree is in English and Journalism, and my God-given aptitude for communication has served me well in various careers. Growing up, I wrote lots of poetry that alternated between angst-filled and rapturous, which is a good description of how I lived most of my life. Finding balance has always been a challenge. I also started a journal because my therapist and friends told me it was a good way to get to know myself better and grow as a person.

Like prayer, journaling is a way to reflect on the past and get in touch with how God has helped me with difficult times and challenging people. Despite my lifelong interest in writing, I didn't start the regular practice of journaling until my first retreat at Abba House, where it was quiet enough for my mind to slow down and form two consecutive, connected thoughts. Within a few months of that first retreat, my journal became a daily letter to God where I could voice my fears and doubts and express my gratitude for many blessings. Today I think of my prayer life as a three legged stool with each leg an equal component: Scripture reading, spiritual journaling, and Centering Prayer. I have learned that whenever I stop practicing one or two of the three, I become off balance; I am not able to live to my fullest potential.

On that first retreat at Abba House, I only stayed two days and one night. Sister Mary Gen told me that it took most people at least two nights to have a decent retreat: one day to slow down and the next day to really settle in and connect with God. I knew I needed to slow down, but I didn't have the slightest idea how. I smile when I read my journal entries from those early visits because the pages are full of other people's thoughts and ideas, and they show my hunger for spiritual food. I was so eager to learn more about the spiritual life that I read from many books, and the sisters had put together an impressive library. I also enjoyed listening to their teaching tapes: at least I could close my eyes while absorbing those.

On the morning after the first night of my retreat, and on many mornings during future retreats, Sister Libby greeted me with "Did you have a good sleep?" She asked as if she honestly cared. I couldn't remember the last time I had been asked whether I slept well, which I rarely did in those days. I came downstairs to get my breakfast and found her at the table eating Cheerios and reading the paper, both on that morning, and on many that would follow. That consistency was very comforting.

Later that morning, Sister Libby was teaching a weekly Scripture study class in the basement of the house—the Sisters called it the "ground floor" —which was kind of musty but roomy. Every room in Abba House had a distinctive flavor to it, and I would get to know most of them in the next decade, even leading my own classes in some of them. This particular class was very enlightening for me. The topic was the Holy Spirit in Scripture, and I heard about various places where the Holy Spirit appeared in the Old Testament under different guises. Sister Libby's spirituality was invigorating. As she taught Numbers 11, where Moses chose seventy people to receive the Holy Spirit, she said things like "the Holy Spirit is in all of us, not just the prime leaders. The Holy Spirit is not restricted to official channels." She respected the church and its structure even as she challenged assumptions.

During the class, one of the women became adamant that Jesus died for our sins to open the gates of Heaven. She insisted that no one could have gone to Heaven until Jesus rose from the dead. Sister Libby literally snorted at that, stating, "You mean to tell me that Moses and Elijah and all the prophets didn't go to Heaven until Jesus came? That's ridiculous! Some of the church's teachings should not be taken so literally!"

It was during that class that Sister Libby first called me an "educator" after I mentioned that, as a catechist, I had not found anything in my catechetical materials about dogma such as "Limbo" and that there was very little mention of Hell. When she said "Listen to Anne, she is an educator," I was so happy! I felt really important. The people-pleaser in me liked gaining the approval of my spiritual director, but I also realize that being an educator resonated with me as an identity. Looking back now, I see that Sister Libby placed a great deal of value on education, as evidenced by the classes she taught and her own continuing education every summer at Boston College. In the years to come, God used both my people-pleasing and Sister Libby's educational convictions to guide me along a path where I could truly grow in faith, when I ventured into education as a career.

After lunch, I joined the Sisters for afternoon prayer, where I was first introduced to praying the Liturgy of the Hours. I remember feeling somewhat ignorant because I had never seen one of those prayer books and certainly had never prayed the Liturgy of the Hours before. Today I understand that the Hours are a standard method of prayer with clergy and religious in the Catholic faith, but not very common to the layperson.

After much painful work and personal growth, I have become aware of a tendency I have had for most of my life to compare myself to others, a habit that took root in childhood. One of the things I remember about my maternal grandmother—I was named for her and was her close companion during my childhood—was her tendency to talk about the mysterious "they." She frequently said things like "that's what they say." I remember asking her, "Gram, who are ***they***?" but never getting a definitive answer. Unfortunately the childhood tendency to compare myself to others often led to my feelings of ineptitude in new experiences, like praying the Liturgy of the Hours. The sisters were patient in their instruction, however, and I caught on gradually as I repeatedly joined them in prayer.

My journal pages from that first retreat at Abba House contain many names and titles of books that I borrowed from the library and perused in my room. I remember going downstairs, feeling as if I needed to tiptoe because the House was so quiet all the time, pulling book after book from the shelves, and returning to my room with a stack. I felt like I was feasting! I took notes on different ways to pray and suggestions for improving my spiritual life. There was much to learn from many of these books, as well as from the times of prayer, formal classes, even the simple hospitality.

Also evident from my journal is my own deep love for God and a real desire to experience the love that I was becoming more and more convinced He had for me. I recognized that in order to truly feel that love, I absolutely had to slow down. I had many service commitments outside the home that fulfilled me, but often left me tired. I struggled with that (still do sometimes) since my tendency to overdo actually comes out of my love for God. I see that there is plenty of work to do here in order for us to arrive at the Kingdom of Heaven on earth that Jesus spoke of so often.

After that first time away—my first time alone with myself and with my God—I returned home much more peaceful and rested. I felt far more equipped to handle the challenges in my own house, which frequently involved an angry adolescent boy sparring with his baffled father, while another frightened little boy looked on. I was able to act rather than react more often, so that occasionally I became part of the solution rather than a contributor to the problem. The change in me must have been apparent to my husband, because, since then, he has always encouraged and supported my retreats. So from the beginning, my times away have borne fruit. At Abba House I began to develop a beautiful spiritual life that became the core from which I now live. I began to truly fall in love with my Creator.

Second Retreat at Abba House

Like most of my good intentions, my commitment to growing a ***prayer life*** had a fitful start. For the first few years after making that promise to myself, I usually wrote in my prayer journal only when I went on retreat or experienced a particularly notable answer to my prayers. I also used the journal for assignments my therapist gave me to promote healing around certain family issues. But I did make incremental progress in developing my spiritual life. I began to search out a time of day that I could commit to regular prayer. I also visited Sister Libby at Abba House for spiritual direction every month or two. She encouraged me to find daily prayer time by telling me stories about people who had come to her through the years as they struggled to fit time with God into busy family lives. I liked her story about the man who locked himself in the bathroom twice a day to practice Centering Prayer in a chair he set in the bathtub. I remember another story of a woman who would pull her apron up over her face to get desperately needed time alone with God. I respected and desired to emulate those examples, and my own commitment to prayer began to grow as I took small steps; whenever I moved one step toward God, He seemed to take a giant step toward me.

I am very grateful that God paired me with a spiritual director who had a lively and sincere devotion to the His Word. Sister Libby was definitely a woman of the Book, and I am happy that her influence has helped me to become one as well. Her obvious love of Scripture was evidenced by the way she used it in the prayer services she created, the Bible classes she taught, and within the context of her spiritual direction. There were times when I would be having particular difficulty quieting my mind for Centering Prayer and Sister Libby would suggest that I "chew on" a single Scripture verse. One such time, she gave me a sheet with a list of Scripture references—one for each day of a month—dedicated to seeking out Wisdom. I used that reference repeatedly when I ventured into troublesome meditative waters. I finally gave it away to a friend with similar issues, creating another link in the chain that God's Word builds between us.

I returned to Abba House in July of 1995 for my second retreat, following my husband's first retirement. I was not handling his increased presence in our home very well, which was already tense as the result of our older son's anger and rebellion. I responded to the increased tension with very high energy and activity, sort of a "frenzied" mode, spending a lot of time in volunteer activities outside the home. I justified my heightened pace by pointing out the virtue of the activities (church, community volunteerism). As a result, I was still in high gear when I arrived at Abba House. Once again, the pages of my journal during that time are crammed with notes about books and tapes I read and listened to. A lot of my personal journaling centered on a search for answers as to why I felt so driven to keep moving. Through my conversations with Sister Libby I began to realize that I had a lot of fear. During my second retreat I began to allow myself to feel the fear instead of running away from it.

Reading over the various notes I took that weekend, I now realize and am very grateful that many of the "suggestions" I read in those books have become everyday parts of my life. At Abba House, I read several resources on Lectio Divina, the four-part practice of Scripture study that involves reading, reflecting, responding and resting, and began to develop that practice. I read books that described praying with the body: for many years now I have had a daily Yoga practice that is an essential part of my morning prayer time. I listened to a multi-part series on Centering Prayer—God-centered meditation—that repeatedly stated the practice appears simple, but is not easy. I learned that the struggle I had with my thoughts running rampant during Centering Prayer was quite normal. Sister Libby reinforced that by telling me, when I voiced my frustration with my racing mind, to "just show up." It took several years for me to fully believe and accept that my mind works the way God created it to work, so whatever happened when I went to God in prayer was meant to be.

One of the exercises I was led to on my second retreat was credited to Saint Theresa of Avila, in which I wrote a list of all the things that evoked fear and thereby prohibited progress in my spiritual life. When I completed the exercise, I was left with a solid inventory of my fears. I shared some of it with Sister Libby, and we talked about how I could address the fears related to my family. She suggested that I pray for patience, and that it could take years to get some of my "family issues" straightened out. She observed that I often wanted a "quick fix" in different areas of my life. She was quite accurate on both of those points.

Before I left Abba House, I completed another of the book's spiritual exercises: an Ignation-type prayer experience. These exercises are powerful, and I always feel very spiritually connected when I do them. I was led to imagine my center, where God dwells, as a beautiful garden with fragrant flowers, lush plants and a crystal-clear pool inviting me to enter. I stood at the edge of the pool and shed my fears as if they were garments, throwing them into a pile to be burned. I cried as I did this, reviewing my fears one by one and discarding them. I was left defenseless in all of my misery and wretchedness, as I believed God saw me. I cried out to God, "can you love me like this, so weak and afraid?" I heard Him answer "can you let me love you like this?" I wept and entered the pool, went under the water and asked to let my fears be washed away. When I emerged I let the water evaporate on my skin.

One of the great blessings that came out of my times at Abba House was a willingness to be open to different types of prayer. Sister Libby and Sister Mary Gen taught me that there is no "right" way to pray; there are almost as many different ways to pray as there are people on the earth. They demonstrated this tangibly by the different types of prayer at the House. I remember an afternoon prayer service with the sisters where the Liturgy of the Hours was replaced with a chanting tape. I also remember Sister Mary Gen asking me if I prayed with crystals, because she noticed one hanging in my car. At that time I had compartmentalized praying with crystals into a "New Age" box (I was listening to a lot of Christian radio), and assigned it a somewhat negative connotation. Sister Mary Gen said that anything that brought me closer to God couldn't be bad.

On my second retreat at Abba House, I stayed for two days and wrote twenty-three pages in my journal. It is interesting that I dated the pages alternately July 17 and July 18, going back and forth between those two dates with the various entries I made at different times of day. I find this fascinating because of the revelations God has given me regarding time and its passage since I made the commitment to write this story about my spiritual journey with Sister Libby and Abba House. Time is a construct created by humans to bring order to our world. Without it there would be great chaos. But I know I am not the only person who has witnessed the phenomenon of marked time either standing still or passing incredibly swiftly. The specific instances I recall most clearly involve occasions where more time was needed because more love was needed in some fashion. I have sat and watched the minute hand on a clock stay frozen in place as several persons talked about what was on their minds and hearts, and I know that God's hand was in that. Another interesting bypass of time is the amazing refreshment that results in the body, comparable to hours of sleep, when a state of meditation has been achieved for as little as a few minutes. I would wager that most people could name at least one instance in their own lives where they have noticed time bending in some fashion. It is a great confirmation of spiritual truths overcoming natural laws.

Time always slowed at Abba House because I was fully present to myself and the God of my understanding. There was little to distract me except what I sought out, and it was always my choice to do that. The sisters were non-intrusive yet supportive. The space was warm and welcoming. The food was good. The prayer opportunities abounded.

While I was on my second retreat, Sister Libby prepared a prayer service for me that focused on fear and trust. She used Isaiah 49, Matthew 6: 33-35 and Psalm 34. She always used music during prayer, and she chose "Shepherd me O Lord" which we often sang in my parish community. I felt spiritually mothered by both Sister Libby and Sister Mary Gen: warmed and fed by their gracious hospitality. Rested and restored, I emerged ready to return to my home, equipped with practical suggestions for communicating with my husband, compromising more in the family and praying for patience.

One month after the retreat I wrote again in my journal to record the answers to my prayers for more patience. A pattern began to appear in my spiritual life. I would hear someone say something that would sing in my soul and would write about it in my journal so I could remember it. (Thank you, Jesus, for that, as these days my memory seems to be fading more quickly than I ever thought possible!) During the writing I would see a connection between that comment and something in my daily life. For example, when someone once made a suggestion regarding communicating with my parents, which I felt I was not able to do very well at that time, I realized that the root of my discontent was the difficulty I was having with my older son and the loneliness I felt in my attempts to deal with it. Although I was asking for and getting help from a lot of different sources, my husband and I were not seeing any significant progress. I felt frustrated and impatient, and that feeling of "wanting more" spread into different areas of my life, including my relationship with my parents. The suggestion I heard in this area was to recognize every positive interaction I had with my parents and to focus my attention on the positive. The very evening after I heard the suggestion about recognizing and focusing on positive interactions, I received a phone call from my mother who offered to stay with our sons for a few days so my husband and I could get away by ourselves. It was a blessed gift, and we were very grateful. That was the first of many times my husband and I "stole away" for weekends while my mother kept the children, and all of us looked forward to them: my husband and I reconnected and the boys were spoiled by their loving grandmother. Those getaways, combined with our faith in God and love for each other, helped our family grow closer rather than further apart during difficult times.

Along with the increased journaling that I began to do after the second retreat at Abba House, I began to understand that God sometimes speaks to us in dreams. I wrote to God about some of the dreams I was having. The feelings these dreams evoked were strong and often brought me face to face with some reality I needed to face. Because I was paying attention to how God might answer my prayers, I was more observant in every area of my life. In one of my dreams I had left my husband for another man, whom I was embracing on the upper floor of an unfamiliar home. I looked out the window and saw my husband walking away, his shoulders slumped. In the dream I fully felt the awful realization that I had irreparably hurt someone I deeply loved through my self-centered behavior. That dream made me understand the depth of my love for my husband, as well as my responsibility as a marriage partner. When I read about these experiences in my journals today, I realize that God was very near to me at that time, always drawing me closer.

ABBA HOUSE—THE HOUSE OF PRAYER EXPERIENCE (HOPE)

Unless the Lord build the house, they labor in vain who build. Psalm 127:1a

Abba House of Prayer was one of over 100 houses that emerged from a House of Prayer movement that began among women religious in the United States following the Second Vatican Council. Most of my understanding of the House of Prayer movement was gleaned from a book by Ann E. Chester, a sister of Immaculate Heart of Mary (IHM) who played a key role in the movement from its beginning in the late 1960's. Her book, My Journey in the House of Prayer, is a joyful, spirit-filled celebration that provides a first-hand account of the birth of the House of Prayer Experience (HOPE). Sister Ann was a part of that experience from its June 1966 inception at the retreat for the IHM General Chapter where she served as a delegate. The retreat leader, Father Bernard Haring, was a Redemptorist priest with a heart for religious whose busy professional lives left them yearning for time and a place for deeper prayer. During the IHM retreat, Father Haring proposed that at least one house of each congregation be devoted to prayer and that the house also be open to the needs of the local church, including lay people. The Chapter passed an enactment calling for the establishment of a House of Prayer within IHM and for study into the rationale behind it. Sister Margaret Brennan was IHM General Superior at that time, and she was deeply interested in the renewal of prayer. Sister Ann became the secretary of the Founding Committee that was set up to explore the establishment of such houses. She and Sister Margaret were pillars of the HOPE movement, providing a centralized clearinghouse of information on starting a house for all who were interested.

It is difficult to do justice to Sister Ann's book with a brief synopsis. It is alive with the Holy Spirit. When I handed it to a friend of mine who is an energetic healer, she held it in her hands without even looking at it or opening it and said, "I sense such an energy in this book." Indeed, Sister Ann's enthusiasm and passion shines through on every page. It is a joy to read, and very informative as well.

Sister Ann describes in detail the early days of the Movement including the Monroe Conference at the IHM St. Mary Motherhouse in Monroe, Michigan, August 1968. The Monroe Conference was named "Contemplative Living in the Contemporary World," and had been envisioned by Sister Margaret with the goal of fashioning a contemplative center for the needs of the IHM community. HOPE Clearing Center, with Sister Ann as the Coordinator, was borne out of that conference. At the Center, Sister Ann disseminated information on the results of the Conference, writing up to ten letters each day at the beginning. Consensus had been reached at the Conference on the paradigm for a House of Prayer. This was new and exciting ground, and the visionaries were clear that much room was to be left for the Spirit in the subsequent development of the Houses.

At the Monroe Conference, the foundation elements for a House of Prayer were determined: flexibility, openness to the world, and expressive prayer flowing from the charism of the members and the specific needs of the church. It was also clear that the Houses were to be important components of the congregations, but not branches. Instead, they were to be places of prayer where busy religious women and men, as well as lay people, could retreat from their hectic daily lives to a nurturing, contemplative community for prayerful rest that lasted anywhere from several hours to a year or more.

A follow-up to the Monroe Conference was a three-day meeting of the core group with Thomas Merton a few months later. Merton had been invited to the original conference but was unable to attend due to his commitment to another movement, dedicated to reinvigorating cloistered religious communities. Sister Ann remembered him as a warm, lovable person with a quick mind and a gentle spirituality. He cautioned them to "leave room for the little ones" when someone suggested using a psychological screening in choosing members for House of Prayer communities. After spending three days reviewing the results of the Monroe Conference, Merton gave the core group the "green light" indicating they were on the right track.

There was quite a bit of interest in forming these Houses of Prayer from many different religious communities: Sister Ann spent a great deal of time answering letters from communities around the country, while Father Haring spread the word about the IHM House of Prayer study whenever he addressed different congregations. Sister Margaret propelled the IHM into action, and they formed their first House of Prayer model community in 1969. Shortly thereafter they started the Kresge House Orientation Program in Monroe, Michigan, which operated from 1970 to 1980. For several of those years, Sister Ann and Patricia Nagle SSND (School Sisters of Notre Dame) traveled around the country, even into Mexico, to offer House of Prayer workshops, a sort of condensed orientation program for congregations interested in opening Houses of Prayer. In their travels they reached twelve congregations of women, two of priests, and two of brothers, increasing the influence of the orientation program still operating at Kresge House.

At the same time Kresge House opened, the IHM community started their own House of Prayer on the grounds of the Motherhouse in Monroe, Michigan. Sister Margaret Brennan released eight sisters from full-time ministry, demonstrating her commitment to the House of Prayer model. In keeping with Father Bernard Haring's admonishment to the IHM community in 1966 to "do no building—use existing facilities, the simpler and more accessible the better," the sisters constructed their house out of two small buildings and a large barn. The barn was redecorated into a large open space that still resembled a barn but also evoked contemplation with its broad openness. This community was named "Visitation" and remained in operation for a number of years.

As a result of all this foundational work, Houses of Prayer began to spring up quickly around the country, and in other countries as well. A directory of Houses of Prayer published in 1976 listed seventy-five houses in twenty-seven states and seven Canadian provinces. Two years later, the list had grown to 102 and added an additional state, as well as four more countries. Many houses closed within a few years, but some key ones remained open and operative for decades.

Some of the titles for the various conferences and meetings held by the IHM community focusing on the House of Prayer movement provide a good summary of the core values of the houses:

- Prayer, Silence, Simplicity
- Advance Without, Retreat Within
- Be and Let Be
- Contemplative Living in a Contemporary World
- Open to the Spirit, Open to the World

Sister Ann's story of how she came to write her book about the House of Prayer movement twenty years after its inception is an example of how the movement came to be as well—both were guided and directed by the Holy Spirit. She notes that the call to write the story emerged gradually, but she recalls the first inkling of it, one December 13th in the late 1980's, which is also the Feast of St. Lucy, whose name means "light." She realized that her seven years at Visitation Community would be coming to an end soon, and she had no plans for her next ministry. She decided to put the matter into God's hands, invited the Angel Raphael as a Travel Companion and went to sleep trusting that an answer would be provided. The next day she realized, reflecting on wisdom gained through years of prayerful living, that passivity is not an attitude that works well with prayer. She understood that action must always be added to prayer in order to make God's kingdom on earth a reality. Then the idea of visiting key Houses of Prayer struck her, as both a kind of sabbatical and an information-gathering exercise for some possible future writing about the House of Prayer Experience. And so the journey, which led ultimately to the book, was born.

Abba House was one of the "key houses" Sister Ann visited in her travels. She described each house as "unique but offer(ing) the same gift: a place where anyone in search of identity can find a rendezvous with God and with self, the character of the experience colored by its setting..." Here is her New York travel itinerary for 1987-88.

- Abba House of Prayer, Albany
  "a seasoned residence sitting with dignity on a tree-lined street in Albany"
- Still Point House of Prayer, Stillwater
  "a brown farm house marked by a large white cross with a rustic bell tower beside it, set in 33 acres of woods"
- Aletheia, Manhattan, New York City
  "a red brick front, proud to be the first residence on Washington Square, recalling for me the mysterious mazes of the city"
- Westcourt, New Rochelle
  "a rambling historic residence, its winding drive and stone gateway speaking of yesterday's splendor" (Quotes from HOPE, p. 74)

In Sister Ann's recollection of Abba House, she credited the existence of the House to Sister Libby, whom she described as a "determined realist." She was impressed by Sister Libby's persistence and resolve in creating Abba House, particularly her return to school to earn an additional degree in nursing, in order to support the House's maintenance by working nights and weekends. She remarked on Sister Libby's "dogged determination" and ability to capitalize on situations to the House's advantage.

In the book, Sister Ann also recognized that Sister Mary Gen was a partner in the House from its formation, and a key to its success. She noted Sister Mary Gen's ecumenical background—-her father was an Episcopal priest and a doctor who had served Native Americans in the Western United States, where Sister Mary Gen was raised. Sister Ann was also impressed by the relationship between Sister Libby and Sister Mary Gen, how their different personalities, gifts and talents complemented one another in the daily activity of the House.

Sister Ann's visit to Abba House was eagerly anticipated by the community, as referenced in their September 1987 Letter to Friends. (The Sisters started writing an annual letter to "Friends" early in their ministry, using a mailing list they created from people who visited the House. They used their Letter to Friends to communicate information about upcoming program offerings and activities at Abba House, to express their gratitude for ongoing support and to share their spirituality.)

> Our resident guest list for September to December is filling up rapidly. One very special guest will be Sister Ann Chester IHM of Monroe, Michigan, a prime mover in the House of Prayer Movement since the mid-sixties. She is writing a history of this significant movement of the post Vatican II church and plans to spend a month of research in each of several well-established houses. We are honored to have been chosen, and we will welcome a dear friend who trained Libby for this work in 1969-71.

While at Abba House, Sister Ann had the distinctively dubious pleasure of experiencing the blizzard of October 1987, which paralyzed Albany for several days and much of Albany's surrounding areas for up to several weeks. Fortunately, Sisters Libby and Mary Gen had taken Sister Ann on an Adirondack "leaf-peeping" tour the day before, so she was able to view the lovely fall foliage before it was decimated by the storm. Sister Ann also traveled to several Houses of Prayer in Australia and described them extensively in her book. These include Karith, St. Kilda, St. Joseph House of Prayer, Townsville, Najara, Dondingalong, Queen's House and Wellspring.

When she visited Abba House again in 1991 for its twentieth anniversary celebration, Sister Ann reflected on the House of Prayer movement in an interview that was published in the *Evangelist*. She stated that the movement was "among the most unique and important contributions made by women religious to the reform and renewal of Catholic life" and that it was a "radical response to the Second Vatican Council's call for a renewal of religious life." Sister Ann recalled:

> Our prayer life was rather mechanical; the whole Church's was at this time. We would be saying so many prayers each day at a certain time. It was rote prayer; we even called our prayers 'spiritual exercises.' What we needed was a personal relationship with God, and a way to maintain it through silent prayer, vocal prayer, spontaneous prayer and reflection.

My House—Growing a Prayer Life

During the several months between my second retreat at Abba House in 1995 and the next time I stole away to the House in 1996, I became thoroughly enmeshed in the chaos in my home. I was clearly a large contributor to the rising frustration levels my husband and I felt over our older son's erratic and sometimes dangerous behaviors. While at Abba House in 1996, I journaled a lot about my self-loathing at joining in the chaos. I recognized that I was reacting rather than acting, and desperately wanted to change.

Anxious and fearful about leaving my husband and two sons alone while I was on retreat, I made the mistake of calling home to see how things were going. With my level of entanglement at its peak, I heard the panic in my husband's voice at the most recent events in our house and his inability to control them. Feeling frustrated and powerless, I jumped into an argument with him. When I got off the phone, I journaled about the anger and frustration I felt at my inability to control my husband's reactions; much the same as I felt about my own reactions while in the midst of the crisis du jour. I was very frightened by many of the events in our home, and instead of focusing on my son's behavior; I focused on our reactions. After the phone call, I prayed for guidance. I felt confused and disoriented, almost like I was losing my mind. I wrote about how I could set up a daily Scripture reading for my husband to help him get through this time. In those early years, I was always coming up with some scheme to help my family deepen their spiritual lives. Then I remembered I was in a **House of Prayer** and resolved to pray about the issue. Whew!

Wisely bringing the focus back to the only person I could change—myself—Sister Libby led me to a spiritual exercise. This was an inventory of both my positive qualities and faults in the past, present and future: I listed qualities and faults I had five years ago in one column, qualities I had at that time which made me a gifted human being, along with faults I wanted to be rid of in the second column and qualities I hoped to have five years later in the third column. Examining the faults I had in the past that no longer dominated my life filled me with gratitude and joy. Assessing my gifts and talents allowed me to rest in the presence of God's love through Centering Prayer with greater peace. The entire exercise showed me that all of my life was grace-filled and that I was greatly loved and favored by God. It was a fruitful exercise.

Each time I was at the House with the Sisters I felt God's presence. At the end of the retreat, I returned to my home with a firm resolve to appreciate each moment with gratitude for the small joys in our family life. I also resolved to be more attentive during my Scripture reading, which I had begun to do daily. God has never disappointed me when I am truly willing to invest time in my spiritual practice.

Along with my consistent daily Scripture reading and my intermittent Centering Prayer, I continued to attempt to write in my journal on a nearly daily basis. In July of 1996 I wrote about how diving into the Word each day gave me great insight into my own life.

> Trying to make my morning reading more of a "lectio divina" I reach for a phrase from the Bible and emerge with "The bruised reed he will not crush, the smoldering wick he will not quench." How often I have felt like a bruised reed, when my willfulness leads me to relationships and situations where I suffer. How easy it is to fall into the mode of victim, crying, "what did I do to deserve this treatment?" In hindsight I can see how, in many cases, my choices led me further along destructive paths: how I was given options at many crossroads in relationships where I could have easily extracted or distanced myself

> but did not. Instead, I was more likely to forge blindly on, without acknowledging or examining my choices.
>
> When I close my mind to God and his tender, passionate love for me, I close my heart as well. I cannot hear him crying that I don't deserve to suffer. I cannot claim the inheritance of love and strength that is mine. I cannot bend to pick it up because my back is stiff with pride and foolish conviction. Like a child, I plug my ears and cry loudly so I do not hear the thunder of his love for me.
>
> Until I am so bruised and exhausted by my thrashing about that I am hopeless and helpless. Truly a bruised reed, I fall to my knees and open my arms and He is there. Once more, amazingly, I am lifted, held, comforted, rocked and caressed like the child of God I truly am.

My spiritual life was deepening, but I continued to stop and start my practice of Centering Prayer. Occasionally, I would experience that familiar deep contentment that felt like bliss, similar to falling off a great height with no fear of ever hitting the bottom. More often, I struggled with incessantly racing thoughts. However, God had drawn me in with the good stuff, so I knew I was on the right track by attempting to continue to pursue meditation. I often heard Sister Libby's voice in my mind when I became discouraged, reminding me to "just show up."

During this time I wrote in my journal about feeling like I was being "de-programmed" in my professional career. After I graduated from college in 1981, I held several positions of increasing responsibility in communications within the private sector before taking a professional traineeship in the public sector in 1987. I had always felt that I needed to be "moving up" some invisible career ladder, making more money and taking jobs with progressively greater prestige and salary. But as I matured in my spiritual life, my mindset changed gradually. Recognition from co-workers no longer fulfilled me as it had in the past and I searched for more meaning outside of the work world. I began to attempt live a God-centered life in all areas, as I tried daily to put His will before my own.

In August of 1996, I once again "retreated" to Abba House. This retreat was very special because Sister Libby and I were alone in the House, and we spent a lot of time together. We talked about Scripture and she answered many of my questions. I felt as if I were "sitting at her feet" and learning from her. We talked with candor about our relationship, too. I told her that I sometimes found her honesty—which she prided herself on—to be rather brutal. She chided me about my projections for a frightening future for my son, saying that I had a tendency to superimpose my own experiences onto others. Sister Libby understood the power of words and she was wisely warning me not to let these family situations turn into self-fulfilling prophecies. She also warned me to be careful of sharing my thoughts and opinions about others too freely, because my words could color other people's perceptions of the people I talked about. What she was honing in on was my tendency toward judging others, which often leads to gossip, both of which I had difficulties with at times. Hearing her honest admonitions enabled me to see myself more realistically. Eventually, with her support and Abba House as a place of retreat and renewal, I was able to increasingly connect with the source of love that would help me to begin to let go of these negative characteristics.

Abba House—Building a Network of Support

Beloved, let us love one another, because love is of God; everyone who loves is begotten by God and knows God. 1 John 4:7

Abba House, circa 1973, (left to right), Sister Mary Gen, Sister Mary Clare Smith OSA, unidentified guest, Sister Libby

From 1973 to 1978, although the Abba community had moved from Kenwood to Western Avenue, Abba House operated with a considerable amount of input from the Provincial team of the Society of the Sacred Heart, which was the RSCJ governing body, as well as from their fellow sisters in the Order. But the physical distance that separated them from the practical support of the community led the sisters to realize that they needed to develop their own support system. In 1978, the sisters developed an Advisory Board composed of laypersons and representatives from both the Roman Catholic and Episcopal dioceses of Albany, as well as the RSCJ Provincial team. The Board was created to assist Abba House in the development of its ministry and in identifying ways to serve the community at large. In September of 1979, Abba House incorporated, and the Advisory Board became a Board of Directors with thirteen members; one member from 1979 to 2001 was BJ Costello, the attorney Sister Mary Gen worked for in the 1970's, who handled many of the legal aspects of the House's operation through the years.

A few years after its formation at Kenwood, the Community began writing "Letters to Friends" to keep supporters of the House updated on activities offered at the House. Their September 1979 letter stated "With the encouragement and approval of the New York Province of the Society of the Sacred Heart, the Board is taking over the administration of Abba House, including ownership of the house itself and total financial responsibility, by June 1980." With the assistance of the Board, the Sisters launched a campaign to raise the $40,000 they would need to purchase the house at 647 Western Avenue from the Society of the Sacred Heart. This fundraising effort may have appeared daunting, since thousands of dollars were needed, but nothing stopped the Sisters. At that time their Community consisted of Sister Libby, Sister Mary Gen and Episcopalian religious Sister Mary Clare Smith. (They also usually had several other religious sisters or laypersons living at the house for extended sabbaticals at any given time.) Sister Mary Clare was an artist who painted icons, and she spent five years at Abba House. Their September Letter to Friends stated "We hope that all of you whom we have served during the past eight years will be willing to help us in our exciting new endeavor. If you can make some personal sacrifice, let it be done as an act of faith in the importance of prayer and the ministry of prayer, as well as of spiritual assistance and sharing in the life of the Lord who loves us."

By May of 1980, they had raised $12,000 of the necessary $40,000, by applying for grants, asking for monthly pledges, requesting one-time donations and contributions of labor to make necessary repairs for household upkeep. The Board of Directors purchased the House from the Society of the Sacred Heart in 1980. Local deacon John Novak, who later became the auditor for Abba House's monetary records for many years, helped arrange the mortgage, with assistance from BJ Costello.

Reverend Bob Limpert was an Episcopalian priest at Barry House and knew the Sisters through their relationship with Father Paul Roman and Barry House. Reverend Limpert was president of the Board for a term during the 1980's, after the House had been purchased from the Society. He noted that the first Board had "done all the work" of acquiring the property and coordinating the initial renovations needed in the House. When he joined the Board in the 1980's, its role was primarily to support the sisters. He said that it took him a while to understand that the function of the Board was to nod and affirm that the Sisters were doing a good job. (I could relate to that—when I first joined the Board I thought there would be more work to be done, but soon found that we were more supportive than contributive.) Reverend Limpert remembers the Board as "a really neat group of people who were very supportive of the sisters and the programs they were putting on. They were a very pleasant group of people."

> *"I remember a Halloween party at the House where we were all in costume and no one knew who we were. It made for great fun."*
>
> *Reverend Bob Limpert*

About the House

Structures where there has been a lot of prayer are different: somehow the very walls seem to absorb the sacredness. Anyone who has noted the peculiar atmosphere of a house of worship, particularly when there is no worship occurring at the time, is aware of this. During my conversations with individuals who visited the House when Sisters Libby and Mary Gen were living there, I was struck by the number of people who commented on the sense of peace and calm they felt upon entering the House.

Helene Conroy, who was very involved with Abba House for many years in various capacities, considered the House "a refuge from the world." She was also in touch with the aura of the House. She recalls, "As soon as I entered it, the stillness entered me. I believe the Holy Spirit was present in every inch of that House. I felt safe there, I felt focused there." Patricia Crewell was another Friend of Abba House who sensed the grace there. She remembers, "Abba House was a remarkable place. It had a special air—you felt as soon as you entered the house—because a contemplative community lived there. " Justine Guernsey remembers Abba House as "a place of peace. You knew God was there." Anne Snyder, who enjoyed many times of prayer and fellowship at the House, summarized it well: "There are places where grace abounds and Abba House was one of those places."

Abba House also had a homelike atmosphere. Walt Chura, who led numerous programs at the House over the years, recalls that the old house had a lot of character and personality, with its beautiful woodwork and sense of history. The structure of the House made it more like a "Home of Prayer" rather than a House of Prayer, according to Walt. "It felt like a home: there was nothing institutional about it. There was an intimacy during the programs there that is not found in a retreat center: that opened people up in ways that a less warm environment would not."

Donna Schneider was one of many people who lived at Abba House for extended periods, on two separate occasions. She calls her times at Abba House "the most important stops I made in my spiritual journey." She came to the house on the recommendation of a Religious Sister of Charity of Halifax from her home parish in British Columbia, Canada, who had spent a sabbatical at Abba House. Donna had been working as a teacher in the public school system and was becoming somewhat disillusioned. She found Abba House to be the perfect place to reflect on where she had been and where she was going. After four months at Abba House Donna concluded that she should continue working with young people, although in a different capacity. She returned a few years later for another extended stay, then visited the House annually for the next fifteen years, according to Sister Mary Gen Smyth.

Another person who lived at the House for a time was Jeanne Ehrlich (now King), who came from the Bruderhof community in the Catskills to attend the State University at Albany. Jeanne told me that her parents were looking for a safe place for her to live during the week while she finished her last three semesters at SUNY Albany. They asked the campus minister about places that might be alternative housing possibilities and were told about Abba House.

The Sisters welcomed Jeanne into their House during 1983-84, and she has very fond memories of her time there. She remembers instantly connecting with Sister Libby at their first meeting. She also remembers a wonderful sense of community and fellowship in the House. She loved both Sister Libby and Sister Mary Gen very much and still recalls by name a number of the people who came through the House. Although she didn't attend Mass, she enjoyed getting to know the priests who came to the House, as the community ate dinner together. She noted the focus of the House, on prayer and connecting to each other and to God, and saw firsthand how the Sisters helped many people to do that. Jeanne's quote from the Memory Book that I put together as the Sisters were leaving Abba House in 2001 follows.

> When I was a student at SUNYA, 1983-84, Abba House provided a wonderful home away from home. Coming from the Bruderhof, a Christian community of families, I immediately felt at home in the "community atmosphere." In addition, the quiet and serenity of the house was not only a great study environment, but taught me to appreciate times of disciplined quiet. The friendship we made 20 years ago has continued until now, and I will always remember Abba House with gratitude and affection. Sister Libby once said to me, "If you don't spend time with God, how do you expect to get to know him?" I've always remembered these words, and will pass them on to my six children.

Following is a quote from the Abba House Memory Book from Stan and Hela Ehrlich, Jeanne's parents.

The nature and the occasion of our encounters with the sisters were all different from each other, but the warmth of the meeting, the support received, their warm humor, and the love felt in every situation were always the same.

The sisters gave a home to our daughter during her University years in Albany, and they offered me shelter and comfort at a moment of shock and exhaustion. They opened their house to the brothers and sisters of my community when we had patients at Albany Medical Center Hospital, and supported us with their prayers. By their love and respect for our community, they gave us the invaluable sense of peace and togetherness in the love of Christ.

May these insufficient words convey the thankfulness of my community of the Bruderhof, of my family and of myself, for having been blessed by Sister Libby's and Sister Mary Gen's presence and service of love in our lives.

"It was a blend of cooking, cleaning, praying, laughing, music—like a real home. The afternoon and evening prayers together were very special. All in all, Abba House was a great place for me to grow and learn."

Donna Schneider

A number of people considered Abba House a "home away from home." The sisters were very welcoming to friends of the House who traveled to Albany from out of town, always encouraging them to spend the night when business or pleasure brought them to the city. Reverend Bob Limpert was one such person. He remembers staying at the House when something was going on in Albany that he needed to attend and says that being with the sisters was "like coming home because he already knew them quite well through their affiliation with Barry House." He even recalls house sitting for them once when they went on vacation. Another person who considered Abba House a "home away from home" was Deacon Nancy Hanstine, who was introduced to the House by Reverend Limpert. She lived on the Pennsylvania border, 121 miles away from Albany, and was studying to become an Episcopal Deacon. Her husband would pick her up from the school where she taught, then drive her the 121 miles to her class at the Cathedral of All Saints, before driving her all the way back home. They always had the assurance that they could stay at Abba House if they got snowed in. The Sisters even gave her a key to the House and invited her to stay there anytime she wanted. She felt very much at home at Abba House—very welcomed.

Entering the House

The act of entering Abba House was a contemplative experience, on those occasions when I allowed myself to be fully present. I entered in three stages, and the physical act of entering mirrored my interior movement toward the rest and peace I found there.

There was limited parking on the city streets in the quiet residential neighborhood, but like the Bible stories of the oil and flour in the widow's jar that never ran dry or the loaves and fishes that Jesus fed the crowds, there always seemed to be just enough parking to accommodate guests. The back entrance on Homestead Avenue was the primary point of entry, although the modestly lit Abba House sign was at the front of the House, which faced Western Avenue. Depending on whether I parked on the street or in the driveway, I had to ascend one of two flights of stairs leading to the back porch. As I climbed those stairs, I usually took a deep breath and slowed my steps, knowing I was entering into quiet and rest. Most seasons, there ware flowers and/or plants in that area to peruse, as Sister Mary Gen was attentive to the landscaping. Then another small set of steps led up to the porch door, which the Sisters kept locked. I had a forced pause there after ringing the bell, as I waited for one of them to open the door, which gave me the opportunity for another deep breath, along with the realization that I was entering a prayerful space and time. Then the inside hall door would open, and either Sister Mary Gen or Sister Libby would take the few steps across the porch to the door where I stood. With a kind word and a smile, I would be drawn into the house on a current of grace and love, through the back porch and into the foyer. When I crossed the threshold of the House and the heavy wooden front door closed behind me, and my jacket was removed and hung in one of the hall closets, I took my third deep breath and let go of my world's tension, knowing I was safe. Then I would begin to allow the peace of the House and its dwellers to settle into my soul.

Abba House Now

When both sisters left Abba House in 2001, the Board of Directors amended the constitution to include a proviso that the house would be returned to the Society if it had to close. That eventually happened in 2006, and now Abba House is home once again to a group of retired RSCJ's. Although the house has been extensively renovated, it retains the air of prayerful peace and joy it had when it operated as a House of Prayer.

My House—A New Focus for the Holidays

In the fall of 1996, Sister Libby asked me if I would be interested in giving a presentation on group prayer experiences at Abba House, as part of a series they were doing on prayer. This would be the first of several presentations I was to make at Abba House. The Sisters often asked regular visitors to the House—people whose spirituality they came to know—if they would give talks. Since everything the Sisters did was grounded in prayer, most of their encounters bore spiritual fruit.

During that same time, my home life was becoming more difficult. As the result of our older son's increasing challenges with academics and following school rules, we had arranged for tutoring and counseling; both of these ratcheted up the stress level at home since he was extremely resistant to any form of help. Each appointment we attempted to bring him to ended in a battle as he argued, raged, sulked, and/or left the house when it was time for us to transport him. He was fast approaching his 13th birthday in December of 1996, a tough age for anyone, but harder for him (and us) because of what appeared to be his poor choices and inability to learn from his mistakes.

The day leading up to my evening presentation at Abba House was like most days in our house—stressful and with crisis looming—although I am blissfully forgetful of the particulars. I wanted to cancel the program, but my husband encouraged me to follow through. I was extremely glad that I did, because it was a wonderfully affirming evening. Several of my good friends from Our Lady of Mercy attended, as well as a few other individuals. It was a cozy but warm and receptive group. I opened the program with an excerpt from the animated film "The Lion King." It was the song "The Circle of Life" during which the baby lion Simba is anointed by the wise old monkey Mufasa and presented to the animals of the kingdom. My theme was "connectedness." I talked about different group prayer experiences I had participated in or designed. It was a new experience for me to share my spirituality with others in a formal setting, as a group leader, and it sparked something deep inside. I felt deeply peaceful and very joyful at the same time. I returned home invigorated by my comfort and ability with this new skill, as well as warmed once again by the hospitality and love of the Sisters at Abba House.

****

For some time I had been experiencing increased menstrual pain, at more than the usual one week out of each month. The pain was so intense one particular time that I visited my gynecologist, who diagnosed an ovarian cyst. However, as the pain became more frequent and eventually nearly constant, endometriosis was suspected. In October I underwent a laparoscopy, and the diagnosis of endometriosis was confirmed.

My prayer life was the glue that held me together. I was writing to God daily in my journal, pouring out my deepest desires and prayers. An entry from November 1996:

> I pray for the wisdom to understand that everything happens for a reason.
> To know that God loves me and wants the very best for me in all things.
> That although it sometimes seems as if He's killing me slowly, He's really helping me grow into the person I'm meant to be.
> Pray that I'll see with the eyes of faith the divine plan—perhaps get a glimpse of the patchwork of my life and how these pieces that now seem so raggedy will one day fit into a lovely pattern.

Pray for the grace to love better, more strongly and fully without expectation or hope of payback.
Pray for the wisdom to meet life's difficulties with grace and hope.
Pray for hope to keep on in love.

The Christmas holidays were fast approaching and I was on the verge of once again getting sucked up into my annual vortex of shopping, baking, and wrapping. For me, the chaos started at Thanksgiving and swept through my older son's birthday in early December, extending to New Year's Day when my husband prepared an extravagant meal for his adult children and their families. My husband is much older than I, and at about the same time we married, his five adult children also began marrying and having children. I love all my step-grandchildren very much, and have always tried to remember each of them in a special way at Christmas. When they were small, it made for a lot of shopping, wrapping and shipping, since half of them live far away.

So, although my motives have always been good, somewhere in all that busy-ness I began to lose touch with what Christmas was all about. When I began paying greater attention to my spiritual walk, I started to look for ways to make the holidays more of a remembrance of Jesus' birth than an opportunity to give gifts to those I love. In my journal, I recorded incidents throughout the holiday season that were special and memorable—times for which I was particularly grateful, like a nice visit with one of my step daughters and her family, and the love and appreciation of my children on Christmas morning.

In the midst of that busy holiday season, when I was feeling particularly overwhelmed, I began a spiritual practice that I still use and which has brought much gratitude and peace to my life: *asking, receiving, recording and thanking*. When I wrote my "note to God" in my spiritual journal in the morning, I asked for assistance in some area of my life. On one of the first occasions I followed this practice, I asked God for direction during the day and the grace to remember to call on Him often as I went about my daily affairs. I prayed to be able to slow down and get in touch with Him. The next day, I wrote about how my prayers were answered.

From the start, the results were amazing! After asking for direction and grace from God that morning, when my son started yelling in response to my request that he leave his video game and join us in the kitchen at the dinner table, I felt an amazing calm come over me. That calm kept me from raising my voice in reply to my son's anger. That calm spread to my husband so that neither one of us responded when our son attempted to initiate an argument. Because no one wanted to argue, our son gave up his fight rather quickly. This was especially significant because it happened to be the day we bought and put up the Christmas tree, which can be a stressful day in any family! I saw the calm and peace in my house as an immediate, tangible answer to my prayers, and vowed to repeat this prayerful practice of *asking, receiving, recording and thanking*.

Reading journal entries from my life's most stressful times reminds me of the many ways God has come to my assistance, particularly at the times I asked. My journal has provided enormous blessings and has raised my gratitude level immensely, giving me the strength and courage to carry on when life is complicated and confusing.

During this particular holiday season, I also learned and grew by observing how Sister Libby and Sister Mary Gen celebrated the holidays, with prayer and friends, and by slowing down and really celebrating the season. They told me about their annual New Year's Eve prayerful gatherings. Sister Libby would prepare a program for the evening that consisted of Scripture readings, prayer responses, silence, and music. Although I was never able to attend one of those gatherings, Sister Mary Gen told me that the programs prepared by Sister Libby were always connected to current events. People would start arriving at 9 pm for the program at 10 pm. Then the Sisters encouraged the guests to go off in the House by themselves for some quiet time and return to the basement, which they called the Ground Floor, for midnight Liturgy. Mass was followed by refreshments upstairs, then fellowship until about 2 am.

The Sisters' traditions made me long for a prayerful holiday in my own home, as I began that year to be more mindful of how I spent my time. In the years to come, I would introduce new practices into our family that helped us to get in touch with the true meaning of the season, many of which created sweet memories that we still talk about when we gather for the holidays. I am particularly grateful for our tradition of praying before and after we open our gifts together. We have a prayer dedicated specifically to the occasion that was given to us during a Generations of Faith program at Christmas one year in our parish. Each year, when we read the prayer, I am so grateful for my family and the love we share for each other and for God.

During that December of 1996, I noted and mindfully celebrated the feast of the Holy Family for the first time, which always falls on the Sunday after Christmas. I love how this holiday celebrates the family, and even though my own family was going through a period of strife and I was in physical pain from my own chronic health condition of endometriosis, I was truly grateful for the blessings of my husband, two sons and numerous stepchildren and their families. I knew that I had a very good life.

ABBA HOUSE—DAILY LIFE/ PRAYER AT THE HOUSE

When I created the outline for the different sections of this book that focus on the ministry of Abba House, *Daily Life at Abba House* and *Prayer at Abba House* were two separate sections. But in the process of my research, I realized that these two topics were inextricably intertwined. This connectedness speaks to how the Mission/Vision and Goals of the House were lived out, and is also reflected in the following excerpt from "Abba House of Prayer: To and From the Center" by Brother David Steindl-Rast, which he delivered at the ten year anniversary of Abba House.

> The life-center or heart which furnishes the required energy for this [house] is the quiet prayerfulness of the community and a spirit of warm hospitality and friendship. Members and guests pray together twice daily, and friends or neighbors sometimes join in. There is a leisurely evening dinner hour with much sharing. These things are very important because persons spend various lengths of time here from a few minutes to a few months, and the prayer and community love are what make a cohesive whole out of an otherwise constantly changing human situation—challenging, yes, but infinitely enriching and broadening—a piece of today's world with all its various features.
>
> *"A few minutes or hours or days of quiet time here with the Lord are the greatest gift we have to offer you. Don't*

> *become too busy to use this! It was once suggested that we should tithe (10%) of our time as well as our money for the Lord. Think of the implications!" September 1992 Letter to Friends*

The sisters brought back to Abba House—figuratively, and sometimes literally—the people they encountered and the experiences they had in their employment and in their parish work; all were lifted up and prayed for. And so, their work "in the world" helped their ministry within the House to grow, extending tendrils of prayer throughout the community.

By 1979, the Abba Community had further defined itself as a "praying community," and identified its ecumenical charism. From the September 1979 annual Letter to Friends:

> The Abba House community is an inter-congregational and ecumenical group of religious women with a continuing and ever increasing ministry to lay persons, priests, and religious sisters and brothers. We offer time and space in our home for quiet and reflection, guidance and support in prayer, private retreats, directed retreats, spiritual counseling, classes in Scripture, individual talks on Scriptural topics, and days of prayer or retreats for groups. Our ministry is the normal outgrowth of our own serious commitment to personal and daily communal prayer which you and your friends are welcome to share whenever you can.

A lengthy article in the June 1979 monthly newsletter on prayer, "The Crux of Prayer," produced by Clarity Publishing, featured Abba House. Sister Mary Gen was quoted as saying that there was an "un-remarkableness" about living in a House of Prayer after one had been there for awhile. She spoke about the way they led their guests to and through their own personal prayer experiences: "We do not offer elaborate programs, but guide people experientially by inviting them into our own group prayer twice a day and helping them individually when they wish. It is a question of learning to pray by doing it, but doing it in a loving, supportive prayerful atmosphere."

Ten years later, the Sisters' annual Letter to Friends in September of 1989 offered the following description of daily life at the House that included ample work time interspersed with regular prayer time:

> By mid-morning the two of us are usually at our desks preparing classes or talks and taking or making phone calls. On one morning recently many calls came—one form a person with a prayer request, one from a Lutheran pastor asking ideas for a newly created prayer group, one from a person seeking spiritual direction, one concerning an event of the Capital Area Council of Churches, one from a fellow committee member doing a project for the Catholic Ecumenical Commission. Calls were made to several priest friends to arrange for liturgies in the house, a publishing house to order books for a fall course, a retreatant to confirm dates of registration, and a repair man for our furnace.
>
> Other paperwork goes on also, divided according to our personal aptitudes. For Mary Gen this means bookkeeping and financial matters, word processing of all outgoing materials on the computer, artwork and photography for brochures, etc. For Libby there is the correspondence with prospective guests and sabbaticals, the composition of press releases and other publicity, fundraising every spring, and work for ecumenical organizations to which we belong.
>
> The days are full, varied and stimulating with lots of contacts with God and all His beloved people. Each of you is remembered at times of intercession as well as brothers and sisters all over this nervous world. We believe our lives impact upon it in some mysterious way in the heart of God. Please support us in prayer too.
>
> Devotedly in Christ,
Libby Hoye, RSCJ
Mary Gen Smyth, RSCJ

The Sisters' annual Letter to Friends in September of 1995 aptly describes their open hospitality.

> ...we would especially like to encourage greater use of this peaceful, accessible house and chapel for private quiet time—a few minutes, hours, days or weeks. Programs are about learning and studying, discussing and doing, but ultimately life is really more about being and about being with God! You may arrange to come at your own convenience and if you wish, we will help you use the time well. Furthermore, there will be time set aside for the purpose of retreats and quiet time beginning on the last Saturday of each month and for the days of the week that follow. Come for as many days as you can at that time (or at another time if more convenient).

****

Following is a reflection of my own personal experience with the House, which I visited frequently in the 1990's.

An atmosphere of quiet was encouraged in the House unless a program was being conducted, such as a Bible Study or other type of gathering. The peace of the House emanated from the prayer that occurred there. The Sisters prayed together in the afternoon and evening, praying the Liturgy of the Hours and reading Scripture and other spiritual books. They also took turns choosing the music that was used during communal prayer, although in latter years, as Sister Mary Gen did more of the physical work around the house, including all of the cooking, Sister Libby selected most of the music. They invited many priests, including Bishop Howard Hubbard, on a regular basis to celebrate Mass in their sitting room and then join them for dinner. They had spiritual programs for lay people and religious which were warm and prayerful gatherings, both during the day and in the evenings.

> *"Abba House is immersed in quiet . . . free from the chatter of television and radio. Everything is oriented to support quiet prayer."*
>
> *Excerpt from 11/7/91 Evangelist article "Abba House of Prayer marks its 20th"*

There was a rhythm of "be-ing" at Abba House different from anywhere else I had been before or have been since. First, there was the energy of the House itself, which was a reflection of the energy of the women who lived there. It was deep and full, palpable upon entering. It almost felt like the air was hugging you when you walked in the door. If you knocked, you were always greeted by one of the sisters, someone who was staying in the House on retreat or sabbatical, someone volunteering for an activity, or a Board member there on business or pleasure. Regardless of who let you in, you could be sure that person was acquainted with the mission of the House. So there was a prayerful, steady consistency, which was beautiful.

When on retreat or sabbatical, guests rose at will from their private rooms and came downstairs to the kitchen for a "pick-up" breakfast. If you were an early riser you might run into Sister Mary Gen who often walked to a morning Mass at a nearby parish. If you slept until 8 or 9 you were more apt to see Sister Libby at breakfast. Guests helped themselves to cereal, toast, coffee, and juice and ate either in the dining room or on the front porch, when the weather was warmer. Sister Libby was always willing to share the morning paper.

> *"[The spirituality] of the Society of the Sacred Heart might be described as 'inwardness for the outgoing...It is classic contemplation correlated with this morning's headlines."*
>
> <u>The Society of the Sacred Heart: History of a Spirit</u>,
> *Margaret Williams, RSCJ, p. 34*

After breakfast, the morning yawned, open and free. If the weather was pleasant, there was the possibility of a walk in the neighborhood or to nearby Buckingham Pond. The library was stocked with a diverse selection of interesting books and tapes. The quiet of the House encouraged prayer and meditation, whether in one's room, the chapel, living room, library or other shared area.

Lunch was also "pick-up" followed by afternoon prayer with the sisters. That was a special time with the Liturgy of the Hours, music, Scripture, peace. After prayer, everyone went their separate ways, reuniting at dinnertime, which one of the sisters prepared. By the time I started coming to the House, Sister Mary Gen had taken over the cooking due to Sister Libby's health limitations, but during most of their ministry they rotated meal preparation. The food was always healthy, flavorful and well-prepared. After we all cleaned up together, we retired to the living room for evening prayer, another special time together, or perhaps there was an evening Bible study or prayer gathering. After the prayer or program, there was always socialization before we retired to our separate rooms.

It was a grace-filled, gentle rhythm, very different from MY house! I loved being there.

> *"I have learned to make prayer my life. I hold a grip onto God, and I know that He is always with me. Work can be a prayer; whatever I'm doing, I'm praying."*
>
> *Sister Mary Gen, from 11/7/91 Evangelist article, "Abba House of Prayer marks its 20th"*

Abba House—Mission/Vision and Goals (revised 9/84)

My house shall be called a house of prayer for all the peoples.
Isaiah 56:7

From the Abba House archives, following are the formal Mission/Vision and Goals/Objectives/Purposes of Abba House during the period from 1984 to 2001.

Abba House is called to be an easily accessible center of prayer in ordinary residential surroundings at the heart of today's local church. Service and activity of all kinds become so demanding that people tend to lose perspective and a sense of meaning. They need support in relating deeply to God, setting priorities, and keeping things in balance.

Abba House is also called to be a center of hospitality and interaction of laity, clergy, religious of different congregations, persons of all ages and backgrounds. Graced with a particular ecumenical outreach, it embraces in its life and work persons of several different denominations and creeds. Aware of the imperative to work for a more just and peaceful world, it tries to raise consciousness and to energize commitment through prayerful consideration of the Biblical teachings on justice and peace and of contemporary writings that address these issues.

Abba House is called to be a home where all persons can feel at ease in the warmth of God's healing love and abiding care.

Goals, Objectives, Purposes

1. To be a true center of prayer, by which we mean praise and worship of God and active intercession for the dioceses, the church, the world.
2. To be an open contemplative house where persons from all walks of life can come to grow in their own prayerfulness by experiencing the support of a praying, welcoming community.
3. To instruct others in prayer and in the study of the Scriptures by offering the atmosphere supportive of private retreats, the skills necessary to give directed retreats, and various specific ongoing programs such as Bible classes, days of recollection, talks on prayer, spiritual counseling, etc.
4. To serve also outside the house in various parishes, giving Bible classes, days of retreat, talks on prayer, etc.
5. To pray for Christian unity and to witness to it by frequent contacts with persons of other denominations in mutual love and service.
6. To be a source of consciousness-raising for the advancement of justice and peace in this world, through all the means described in goals 1-5.

"Welcome to another year in our mutual search for a deeper relationship of love with our God. Abba House continues to be a place where individuals can come for short or longer periods of quiet time, spiritual guidance, etc. Many of you call here for prayers for special needs and you are most welcome to do so. In return we ask that all of you pray earnestly for us in this beautiful yet highly responsible ministry."

September 1994 Letter to Friends

MY HOUSE—PHYSICAL CHALLENGES

When I began reading the spiritual books Sister Libby recommended, I noticed that one spiritual book would lead to another, which in turn would lead to another. In this way, I enriched my spiritual life while building a nice library of books. One of the books I read was Women's Body, Women's Wisdom by Christiane Northrup, M.D. This book described endometriosis as a competitive disease that occurred when women found their interior desires and exterior work-worlds conflicted. I took my own inventory and got in touch with some grieving around my inability to have a daughter. I also worked on healing several other events that occurred during my childbearing years. There was work to be done, and I am very grateful that God gave me the courage and strength to face several memories from my college years and first marriage that I had been running from for some time. I began to understand the complicated coping mechanisms I had developed, and discovered that one of them was illness. When I was growing up, being sick was a way to get attention. In addition to endometriosis, headaches were another of my chronic illnesses; although I had frequent headaches since I was a teenager, it wasn't until the early 1990's that I was diagnosed with migraines. The neurologists call them "common migraines" but anyone who has ever had one knows there is nothing "common" about them. Mine are triggered by a variety of different events and circumstances, most of them stress-related. When I was dealing with migraines and endometrial pain at the same time, as I was in 1996-98, I often felt overwhelmed. Still, I usually refused to give into the headaches because they made me angry: I medicated myself with triptan drugs and other pain killers and continued going to work and taking care of things that I felt required my attention. Occasionally I would "take to my bed" for a day or so. Fortunately, the frequency of these headaches has decreased over the years, largely due to my work with a homeopath. Progress in healing is slow but definite. But like other "thorns in the flesh" the migraines keep me running to God, which is a good thing.

During January of 1997 I experienced daily, almost constant, endometrial pain during the day, which also woke me nearly every night. An entry in my prayer journal in mid-January reminds me how God breaks through the most difficult times of our lives with His presence. I had gotten back into the practice of Centering Prayer in the early morning, and wrote about an experience that day.

> This morning I dragged myself out of bed to have my quiet time with You, Lord. I was in so much pain that I could not bring myself to center and I cried out to You. I seemed to hear you say, "try again" so I did. Then I felt your Spirit in my center—like a hunger deep in my belly—and that wonderful peace that only You can bring. I also felt a complete absence of pain! As I prayed in silent oneness with You, I wept from time to time and heard "Let them hold you."
>
> I realize that there are many people who hold me as I walk through this difficult time. I need to remember that. Miracles happen so often in my life. If I am not asleep or absorbed in my own issues, I can recognize and thank You for them. I truly am a favored daughter.

It was only when I opened myself up to God that I could I have such beautiful prayer experiences: Similarly, I needed to find *people* I could trust and be open with as well. That day, I carried the phrase I heard in prayer—"let them hold you"—as I went on my way and encountered different people. I was particularly attuned to the spiritual gifts I received from those people. I found comfort in the most unexpected places: in a Catholic school uniform shop where I ran into an acquaintance from the past who was uncharacteristically interested and empathetic, and from a friend who took the time to share her own experiences with her son as he was growing up. I was beginning to truly reap the fruits of the "interconnectedness" Father Roos had talked about during his homilies.

On some level, I knew that *love* was the ingredient that would hold my family together through our difficult times. I bought a throw rug "when you need a hug, stand on this rug" printed on it. I put it in the spot that would become the dog's area when we adopted a Greyhound later that year. All of the guys loved that rug and jumped on it whenever they had the chance, just standing there with open arms, until whoever happened to be closest obliged them with a hearty hug. The rug definitely helped to lighten the mood in the house.

In mid-February, I returned to Abba House for a few days, where I learned more about praying the hours through a book Sister Libby loaned me by Benedictine Brother David Steindl-Rast, called The Music of Silence. When I told her how beautiful I found both the book and the author's spirituality, she informed me that Brother David was the person who had suggested that she start a House of Prayer. She also said that he spoke at both their ten and twenty year anniversaries. During this retreat time at Abba House, I prayed to be able to be a channel of grace and mercy when speaking to my husband, an especially relevant prayer since my retreat was interrupted by a distraught phone call from him; he was having a particularly difficult time with our boys at home.

Shortly after returning home from this short retreat, I had a spiritual experience that affected the entire family. One day I went to work, leaving the boys at home with my husband as they had a school holiday. After praying in the morning, I asked my husband to watch the boys during the day and to notice how much they loved one another. He appeared to think about my words. When I returned in the afternoon, I was amazed at the joy in the house—everyone was so happy! My husband was grinning from ear to ear, sitting on the couch and watching the boys playing on the floor together. I already knew that love could change a lot, but through this event I saw that love recognized and noticed can change everything.

Still, by the time Ash Wednesday and Lent rolled around in March of 1997, my marriage had taken a bit of a nosedive due to the constant pressures of our son's issues and my physical pain. I realized that in order to strengthen our relationship we needed some outside help.

"I'm not happy," I said one night as I was getting ready for bed.

"What do you mean, you're not happy?" my husband asked.

"I'm not happy in our marriage," I said. "Are you?"

"Of course I'm happy," he answered. "Why wouldn't I be happy?"

"You don't act like you're happy. You're always yelling."

"I'm not yelling. I'm raising my voice. You'll know when I'm yelling," he said. That comment never failed to ignite my anger.

"Listen, I'm fifty percent of this relationship. And if I'm having problems, you're having problems, too." I said, raising my voice.

We went to counseling.

That was a great move on our parts, as we have benefitted greatly from the different therapists we have worked with through the years. I have always joked that I could tell my husband something a dozen times and never get much of a reaction from him, but as soon as one of our counselors told him the same thing he would say "Really???" astounded, as if he had never heard it before! Pretty funny, once I got over my initial resentment.

We revitalized our marriage further by going on a cruise together in the spring of 1997. During that time, I saw how much he respected my prayer. Each morning when I wanted to read my Bible, he left me alone in our little cabin. We had a memorable week on the cruise, experiencing many beautiful beaches, interesting cultures and lovely times of relaxation. We were extremely grateful to my parents for watching the children. We returned refreshed, with our marriage renewed, which was good, since it didn't take long for life to challenge us again.

ABBA HOUSE—IN THEIR OWN WORDS

"How Our Ministry Grew" by Sister Libby Hoye, RSCJ

Written by Sister Libby, published in 1996 Evangelist on Abba House's 25th Anniversary

My colleague, Sister Mary Gen Smyth, and I are members of the Society of the Sacred Heart, an international Catholic religious congregation. When we came to Albany in 1971, we wanted to establish a "House of Prayer" which would number among some 150 others worldwide.

We thought we (and the Lord) had one goal in mind for such a center of spiritual and faith renewal: to provide a home-like setting where Roman Catholic sisters, brothers, clergy, and lay people could come to gain time and space for individual and group prayer. We called it Abba House of Prayer.

Looking back from the standpoint of 25 years in this ministry, I see that the Lord also had another idea in mind for Abba House: an ecumenical and interfaith ministry. We believe God drew us into that work through relationships with many people of faith in the greater Capital District.

The first diocesan priest who came to pray with us was just such an instrument of God. He was assigned to teach religious education in five or six small Catholic parishes in the Adirondacks. There, he was graciously welcomed by the staff of three Episcopal priests and a married couple at Barry House, the Episcopal

Diocese's retreat center in Brant Lake. A short time later, the Abba House and Barry House "communities" began to meet, pray together and move along the road to friendship.

In turn, that led to Episcopalians coming to Abba House in Albany for prayer, retreats and programs. In a further development, the Abba House staff was invited to work in Episcopalian parishes, giving "quiet days" (or retreats) and conducting Bible study classes.

Though never before involved in ecumenical ministries, here in Albany, we were truly on our way to being genuine "ecumenists."

Membership on the Albany Diocese's Commission on Ecumenical and Interreligious Affairs opened more doors. Likewise, service as diocesan representative to the board of the Capital Area Council for Churches (which now has fifteen Catholic member parishes) expanded my ecumenical horizons even further.

With Sister Mary Gen also active on ecumenical committees in the area, Abba House gradually found itself welcoming guests from the wide family of people baptized into Christ: Presbyterians, Methodists, Baptists, members of the Reformed Church, and others.

At the same time, contacts with rabbis and Jewish laity began to expand. Likewise, our contacts with leaders and laity of Islam grew, as did our connections with representatives of the Hindu and Buddhist traditions.

Growing out of those contacts, an interfaith program, now annual, has grown up within the past five years at Abba House. We believe it is also distinctive. Here, small groups of interested people can learn first-hand from members of other great faith traditions, often praying together in a home-like setting dedicated to the service of the Creator.

In all these ecumenical or interfaith programs, a basic ground rule is observed: People are respectful, even reverent, of the background and culture of others. Moreover, they leave these events enriched and affirmed in the tradition of their own faiths.

Over these past 25 years at Abba House, I have seen a deepening spirit of faith, hope and love develop, a spirit which is always enriching to everyone involved. And I have learned that

God is clearly at work in all persons who reach out to the Divine and to their fellow human beings in love and service.

We pray that such spiritual enrichment takes place everywhere in God's own time.

My House—More Spiritual Growth

"Mucky times make great fertilizer"

One of the greatest stressors in our home was the difficulty we had in getting our older son to school: many mornings he would not get out of bed. Both my husband and I put a high value on education, and we were distraught, to the point of threats, cajoling, bribery, squirt guns, pots and pans, getting a favorite teacher on the phone to talk to him, driving him to school late, anything to get him up and off to school. We exhausted ourselves over the years, trying all of these tactics.

In spring, I stopped Centering Prayer for several weeks, which I think was due to my fear that God would tell me our difficulties were going to continue for a long time. I believe that I already knew that, on some level anyway, and I did not want to hear that I would learn some valuable lessons from these experiences, which is what I had heard during prayer times on more than one occasion. Instead, I clung to my Scripture reading and spiritual journal-writing, feeling off-balance with only two of the three rungs of my foundational prayer life intact. Even so, my prayer life became my lifeline during that time, which is remarkable, considering I didn't even HAVE a prayer life a few years earlier! And God—my loving, compassionate and wise heavenly Father—was pulling that lifeline toward Him. Slowly but surely, I was being drawn closer through my difficulties, as I was compelled to turn to Him for guidance, support and sustenance. I was developing a deep, personal relationship with God, even as I tried to turn away by stopping Centering Prayer. In the next few months, I stopped and started my meditation, but never, ever missed my morning Scripture reading. The Word was my sustenance, my spiritual food.

When things were chaotic at home, I looked outside for activities where I felt like I could both grow as a person and make a positive impact, so I plunged myself into activity at my parish community. Since our family's financial situation allowed me to work a reduced schedule of three days each week. I usually spent one of my weekday mornings at church, attending Mass and then visiting the "upper room" with my two friends Pat and Irene, who worked at Our Lady of Mercy (their offices were upstairs at the church). Pat and Irene were responsible for the parish Religious Education program, and I had graduated from leading Children's Liturgy of the Word to teaching a weekly religious education class during the school year. During our time together, we prayed, studied Scripture, prepared programs for catechist gatherings, and enjoyed each other's company. They were and continue to be immensely affirming, deeply spiritual and loving friends who have been essential to my spiritual growth.

As my friendship with Pat and Irene grew, I became more involved in Youth Ministry at Our Lady of Mercy. During that time, it was becoming more difficult to convince our older son to attend weekly Mass with the family. I prayed for something at church to help him feel more connected. I served on a Youth Ministry team with Irene, and we talked often about doing something at Sunday Mass that would help the young people to become more involved. I brainstormed with Carol, another team member, and we proposed a monthly Youth Mass, then we reached out to the young people from the religious education classes and solicited volunteers to serve as ushers and greeters. We also enlisted young people to break open the Word of God for the congregation by creating some sort of reflection or skit on the Gospel reading of the week. My older son occasionally served as an usher, but it was clear that this initiative was not much of an answer to my own personal prayers. Yet the Youth Mass did help a few dozen young people stay connected to the church and resulted in some wonderful skits performed by talented young people that the entire congregation enjoyed.

The teenagers who agreed to do the presentations during Mass were willing, fun and very interesting, and they came up with some of the best ideas! One very entertaining session involved several of the students taking on the personas of different disciples as part of a "Phil Donohue talk show" hosted by our parish priest (they even called him "Phil"). Jesus wore a Superman shirt and a beatific smile. Peter was very loud and verbally dominant, repeatedly interrupting the moderator with "Let me tell you, Phil," and describing what ***really*** happened when they were together during those eventful three years. It was very funny, lively and definitely Spirit-filled. One of the other programs involved the kids handing out bags of goldfish crackers after Mass ("go and be fishers of men"). There were also a number of memorable skits where the students acted out scenarios that could have happened in their teen lives. Our adult planning meetings were full of companionable fellowship, love and commitment to our young people. It was a wonderful, fruitful time, both in our church and in my growth as a catechist.

During the same time period, I also sought and found spiritual nourishment at the Cathedral of the Immaculate Conception, which was down the hill from my office at the Empire State Plaza in Albany, New York. The Cathedral offered a daily noon Mass, and I began to attend occasionally. Initially, I remember that I was not sure why I went, but I soon realized that I always felt better about myself, the people in my office and life in general when I returned to work after Mass. Within a few weeks I recalled that I had attended evening Mass during weekdays in Lent when I was a child and had always enjoyed it. I remember being sad when Lent was over and the evening Masses ended, because my school schedule did not allow me to attend daily morning Mass. I found the Roman Catholic Mass to be familiar, comforting and restful. My experience of Mass was enhanced by what I was learning as a catechist: the children's workbooks clearly explained the Catholic Mass as composed of two parts: the Liturgy of the Word and the Liturgy of the Eucharist. I was discovering that both parts equally fed me.

So I was reaching for God in several different areas of my life, and reaping great fruits, primarily in my relationships with others. I was developing deep friendships and finding fellowship with like-minded people on similar spiritual paths. These people popped up in unexpected places and traveled in and out of my life. They have made lasting impressions on me, whether I spent hours, days, weeks or years with them. I was discovering that God does not want us to take our journeys alone.

****

I was beginning to understand the "interconnectedness" Father Robert Roos talked about. Father Roos sometimes said the noon Mass at the Cathedral, had a perpetual twinkle in his eye, and always opened his homilies with a joke, like this one.

"Do you remember the time Jesus drove the multitude of demons out of the possessed man?" Father Roos was tall and slender, and he would wrap his long arms around the Missal, holding it close to his chest while he told his opening anecdote. He continued, "there was a herd of swine grazing on the hillside and the demons rushed out of the man and into the pigs, who became excited and started running wildly. They ran off the edge of the hill where they were grazing and fell into the sea." He turned his head and looked at his small congregation out of the corner of a twinkling eye and said, "that was the invention of deviled ham."

Because of his gentleness and good humor, I asked Father Roos to be my confessor. He was caring for his elderly mother at the time, and I was able to go to their home one evening so he could hear my confession. I only had that one visit with him, but he made a lasting impression. We talked about different people and situations in my life, and he said, "you have a lot of stories." When he found out we knew some of the same people he said, "that is God's wonderful interconnectedness." He said the word slowly, emphasizing each syllable. It struck me, and has become somewhat of a theme in my life.

In spite of my forays into new areas of prayer and spiritual enrichment, I still considered Abba House my home away from home and the place where I went to be alone with God. I met with Sister Libby on an almost monthly basis for spiritual direction, where she would ask me how my prayer time was going. She looked at me with surprise when I told her about some of my troubling encounters earlier in life, and remarked "you've been through a lot in your short life." I am truly grateful that God was calling me into relationship with Him and giving me loving guides like Sister Libby to help me deal with my difficulties: she was a lightning rod for God's love and care.

One of my greatest difficulties continued to be what I then considered to be the rebellious behavior of my older son. I prayed endlessly for answers, and often talked to the sisters at Abba House about my problems. I told Sister Mary Gen that people told me not to think so much. She said that was probably the Holy Spirit talking to me because He could not enter me when I was tense and busy. Sister Libby was always willing to listen to me and acknowledged my difficulties, encouraging and supporting me in my prayer life, suggesting that I try new avenues of prayer. She talked about how the rosary was an excellent meditative prayer because the beads kept our hands busy while the repetition of the Hail Mary's kept our minds from wandering. During this time, I began praying the Chaplet of Divine Mercy, which was also prayed with Rosary beads, but was shorter and easier for me to finish. And the Chaplet was a good way for me to formally cry out for God's mercy, which I felt my family needed desperately.

All of this spiritual seeking nurtured my relationship with God. By bringing my needs to God, recognizing His answers to my prayers daily through journaling, and receiving encouragement from Scripture, I became convinced that my son would eventually work his way through his issues. And he does continue to do so, with the loving support of his family and many other people. St. Paul writes of the great gifts of faith, hope and love. I agree wholeheartedly that the greatest of these is love: God has shown deep love for me which has been delivered by many faith-filled people.

Because of my time apart in prayer and at Abba House, as well as the family situations we were undergoing, I was beginning to define the priorities in my life. In addition to my family and work priorities, being a catechist was definitely a priority. Catechetical experiences at my church were joy-filled times. It felt freeing to be able to talk about God and how much He loves us. Most of the young children I worked with were receptive and responsive to the weekly religious education program I was teaching: First Eucharist Sacramental preparation. I felt like I was planting important "faith seeds" which had great potential for growth throughout each young person's life. I felt privileged to be a part of the faith journeys of these beautiful children.

Contrasting with the happy, fulfilling times of catechesis were repeated unexpected and angry, violent outbursts at home. These eventually led to my own recurrent anxiety, perhaps related to an earlier diagnosis of Post Traumatic Stress Disorder. I was finding it increasingly difficult to navigate the emotional fluctuations in my life.

When the boys got out of school in June, the summer spread out before us like a yawning chasm. Within a few weeks we had to call the Mobile Crisis Unit when our older son's rebellious behavior moved into violence. We were being advised to file a PINS (Persons in Need of Supervision) petition in Family Court in order to bring these issues into the realm of the courts in the event the dangerous behavior escalated. In New York State, filing a PINS petition is a way to bring law enforcement and/or the judicial system into a family's life when the family is unable to deal with the behavior or an un-emancipated minor. I saw it as a last resort and was hesitant to take the step.

We continued to bring our older son to individual counseling and also initiated family counseling, but he wouldn't admit that he needed to change. His teachers had been telling us about times when they saw him doing things that were clearly in violation of school rules, such as stealing and ignoring teacher instructions, but he usually denied them. Later we realized that he was out of touch with reality due to his illness, but at the time, he appeared to be contrary and rebellious, rather than sick. It has always been a fine line for us to figure out how much of his behavior was stubborn defiance and how much was a genuine inability to perceive what seemed to be apparent to everyone else.

Thankfully, I continued to be blessed with exceptional prayer times, like this one that I wrote about in my prayer journal.

> When I went for a walk in the morning, feeling the endometrial pain already that I knew would increase through

> the day, I asked Jesus to join me in the park. We walked together for a while, talking and laughing. At one point He put his arm around me and pulled me close, kissing me on the forehead and squeezing my shoulders. He told me He loved me and that I was doing good things. He made me smile. Later during our walk He ran and played and I watched him, laughing. What a wonderful start to the day! I am going to invite Him along more often.

This was the fruit of learning different ways to pray during my stay at Abba House. I had read about using imagination in prayer, and decided to give it a try. Sister Libby and Sister Mary Gen encouraged all kinds of prayer. It was wonderfully freeing to know that I didn't have to be limited by memorized prayers and rituals.

Abba House—Religious Inclusivity

Ecumenism

Ecumenism was an integral part of Abba House's charism. Both Sister Libby and Sister Mary Gen had deep respect and affection for other faith traditions. As noted in an earlier section, when Sister Libby had been a high school teacher in the 1950s and 1960s, she brought her students to visit houses of worship belonging to other faith traditions, which was not a widespread practice at that time. Sister Mary Gen had been born and raised Anglican, and her father was an Episcopal priest. She converted to Catholicism in her late teens, so she was very aware of the many similarities between the two faiths. When she came to Abba House, she brought with her a natural openness to other faiths.

The sisters worshipped regularly with Anglican friends when visiting Father Paul Roman, a Roman Catholic priest who lived at the Anglican retreat center Barry House while he worked as the diocesan director of Religious Education for six parishes in the Adirondacks. The Anglican and Roman priests living at Barry House alternated celebrating Mass and leading morning and evening prayers. A foldout pamphlet in the Abba House archives from the 1970s was actually a joint flyer for both Abba House and Barry House.

Reverend Delos Wampler was the director of Barry House for 32 years, and he warmly remembers the close relationship between the two houses. He first met the Abba Community when they were still in residence at Kenwood. When they moved to Western

Avenue, Barry House donated several articles to help set them "set up housekeeping," including an altar that was used to celebrate liturgies in the early days, before the sisters began holding Mass in their sitting room. The Abba House sisters continued to attend celebrations at Barry House with Reverend Wampler at Abba House for many years. Reverend Wampler even served as president of the Abba House Board of Directors for several years.

Another Episcopal clergyman with strong connections to the House was Reverend Bob Limpert, who was a priest at Barry House when he met the Sisters through their relationship with Father Roman. Reverend Limpert was involved in the Diaconate (Deacon formation) program and often used Abba House for meetings with candidates in the program. He also referred several women to Sister Libby for spiritual direction. He regularly went to the House to celebrate Mass and eat dinner, and led several programs there, including one on Celtic spirituality. Father Limpert remembered, "ecumenism was different at that time. There was a real openness that lots of times does not seem to exist these days."

By 1974, the Abba Community was welcoming Anglican friends to their house on Western Avenue for prayer and fellowship. When opportunities arose to interact with the Anglican community, the Sisters took advantage of them. For example, the 1974 Abba House Letter to Friends told of Sister Libby leading a day of Recollection at the Episcopal Cathedral. William McEwan, a member of St. Paul's Episcopal Church in Albany, was elected vice-president of the Abba House Board in 1981 and president in 1983. They also extended personal hospitality to the Episcopal community by inviting the Anglican bishop and his wife to dinner.

A significant contribution to the ecumenical charism of the House in the early years was the addition of an Anglican nun to their community in 1976. An article about Abba House in early 1978, written by the editor of the *Albany Churchman*, a publication of the Episcopal Diocese, was also published in the *Evangelist*, a publication of the Albany Roman Catholic Diocese. The daily ecumenism lived out at Abba House was significant in 1978, as noted in the opening paragraph of the article.

> As we look all around us for signs of the Spirit of God moving among us it is often easy to overlook what is right under our nose. What 10 years ago would not have been possible is now a daily reality at Abba Community House of Prayer. Here, in the Diocese of Albany, we have an Ecumenical religious community. Ecumenism is not just a word, nor an occasional occurrence at Abba House. It is a way of life. Abba Community has as its permanent members Sister Libby Hoye and Sister Mary Gen Smyth of the Religious of the Sacred Heart, and Sister Mary Clare Smith, an Anglican sister.

The article also told of how Sister Mary Clare Smith's vows to the teaching order of the Sisters of St. Anne were "quietly received" in a ceremony at Abba House by Episcopal Bishop Hogg. The article noted that the Abba Community had played a significant role in Sister Mary Clare's decision to enter the House of Prayer, as she "had visited the Community many times for extended periods to test her vocation to a life of prayer and reflection." The article went on to describe some of the activities of the Abba Community, both in the house on Western Avenue and in various parts of the Albany Roman Catholic and Episcopalian dioceses. While noting the Community's contributions to areas outside the House, the article stressed prayer as its foundation. The article concluded:

> In a time when we look to Rome or Canterbury for signs of growing ecumenical awareness, it is heartening to find this ecumenical community flourishing in our midst, supported and encouraged by Bishop Hogg and Bishop Hubbard, functioning so well as to be unobtrusive.

An article from the June 1979 *Crux of Prayer* described Abba House as the only "full-time ecumenical (Anglo-Roman) House of Prayer." The shared prayer of the sisters and the many guests who visited the House was a living witness to their spirit of ecumenism. One of the basic objectives of the House at that time was "To pray for Christian unity and to witness to it by our very lives as an Anglo-Roman group of Sisters living and praying together and offering our services in both these Churches."

> *"Abba House was an oasis of prayer within the Diocese that promoted Catholic and Christian spirituality."*
> *Bishop Howard Hubbard*

By 1979, the Abba House community, already heading into its ninth year of operation, was defining itself as an "inter-congregational and ecumenical group of religious women with a continuing and ever increasing ministry to lay persons, priests, and religious sisters and brothers." (September 1979 Letter to Friends) That same year the sisters formed their first Advisory Board, which developed into the Abba House Board of Directors. Further evidence of the ecumenism of the House was demonstrated by the composition of the Board, members of several different Christian denominations, all of whom were handpicked by the Sisters with a love of both prayer and the House as common thread.

Reverend Bob Lamar, pastor of the First Presbyterian Church in Albany, was a good friend of Abba House and a Board member for several years. He went to the House primarily for meetings with the Board, who were there "representing several traditions in the family of faith," as he described them. He believes that Abba House was one of the significant outgrowths of a very fruitful time of ecumenism in the 1960s following Vatican II "when some of us realized that we could talk to each other." Bob had become friends with Bishop Hubbard during the 1960s when they were involved in an interfaith taskforce in the South End, which led to a number of significant social initiatives, including housing, ecumenical gatherings and lectures. He said that all of these initiatives were good, but "what Abba House brought to the interfaith/ecumenical community was their spiritual quality of prayer—they were very specifically centered in prayer and spirituality."

> *"Every time I drive by the House on Western Avenue I glance at it and get a special feeling."*
> *Reverend Bob Lamar*

In 1979, Bishop Hubbard appointed Sister Libby to the Roman Catholic Commission for Ecumenical and Interreligious affairs. That same year Abba House hosted a prayer service themed "Serve One Another to the Glory of God" to mark the annual Week of Prayer of Christian Unity. As noted in the Programs section, many of the formal offerings and prayer gatherings at Abba House reflected ecumenical concerns.

As their ministry continued through the years, the Community's commitment to the ecumenical and interfaith aspects of their ministry grew. A group of women from the local Dutch Reformed Church held days of prayer at Abba House. The Northeast Synod of the Presbyterian Church held planning meetings at the House every few months because they found the atmosphere of Christian hospitality and simple living conducive to their own prayerfulness.

The Sisters' September 1981 Letter to Friends told of new ecumenical involvements with Methodists and Presbyterians and continuing good relationships with the Episcopalian community. The Episcopal deacons met for many years at Abba House. Women ecumenical clergy held support groups often, as Sisters Libby and Mary Gen were very supportive of women clergy in different denominations. There were a number of public events geared toward ecumenism, including a 1985 presentation by Thomas Stransky, CFP, and a Paulist priest who was at the forefront of the movement. Father Stransky was a member of a joint working group for the World Council to Churches and the Roman Catholic Church.

The ecumenical efforts of the Abba Community were noted at their 10th anniversary dinner in October 1981. The speakers were Bishop Hogg of the Episcopalian diocese, Bishop Hubbard of the Albany Diocese and Father Paul Roman, longtime supporter of the House of Prayer. The speakers congratulated the sisters on their House of Prayer ministry, a significant part of which was their ecumenical efforts. Both sisters were active in several ecumenical organizations, including the Roman Catholic Commission for Ecumenical and Interreligious Affairs, the Uptown Churches—an ecumenical fellowship of twelve congregations in the Pine Hills section of Albany—and the Capital Area Council of Churches.

> *"I remember the Sisters of Abba House for their dogged determination and unshaken commitment to promoting Christian unity. They also had a deep spirituality and generous sense of hospitality."*
>
> *Bishop Howard Hubbard*

Kitt Jackson remembered both Sisters fondly, since Libby and Mary Gen were both on the Board when she came to work for the Capital Area Council of Churches in the fall of 1997. Sister Mary Gen was the head of the Prayer and Worship Commission, and Kitt Jackson worked closely with Mary Gen on issues related to that topic, as well as on the Ecumenical Baptism Witness Program. Kitt served as the Administrative Director of the Council, and Abba House was part of the Council as an ecumenical organization. The Sisters advertised their programs in the Council newsletter, and the Council held many of their meetings at Abba House. According to Kitt, "their presence on the Board was much appreciated and valued."

In June of 1987 the sisters took their ecumenism on the road by traveling to the Eastern Ecumenical Conference of the Christian World Mission at Silver Bay, New York where they gave three one-hour presentations on Biblical Images of Shalom. The event was a five-day conference of multi-denominational Christian clergy and laity.

An April 8, 1989 article in the *Albany Times Union* spoke of Abba House's growing ecumenical charism.

> About 20 percent of Abba House's visitors are not Roman Catholic and ecumenical gatherings are increasing. On April 25, for instance, pastors from Protestant churches will join Hoye in a program devoted to the attention given to the Holy Spirit in the prayer life of the different Christian traditions. To join the ecumenical evening of prayer, which begins at 7:30 p.m., call the sisters at Abba House.

In April of 1989 Abba House hosted an Ecumenical Evening of Prayer. The topic was "The Attention Given to the Holy Spirit in the Prayer Lives of our Different Christian Traditions." Speakers were the Reverend Maggie McCarey-Laird, Calvary United Methodist Church, Latham; Reverend Paul Spear Fraser, United Church of Christ, Freehold; and Sister Libby. The following year the Sisters hosted a similar program in May, 1990 with the topic "Gifts that Women Bring to Church Ministry." Speakers were Sister Nola Brunner, CSJ (Congregation of the Sisters of St. Joseph), Vicar for Religious, Catholic Diocese of Albany; Reverend Frances Duffley, Pastor, Zion Church, United Church of Christ, Sand Lake; and Reverend Jennifer Reece, Minister, Emmanuel Reformed Church, Castleton.

In January of 1991 Sister Libby contributed an article to The Evangelist's interfaith column "Our Neighbor's Faith" titled "Building on Commonality." The article commemorated the 25th anniversary of "Nostra Aetate," the Vatican II declaration on the "Relationship of the Church to Non-Christian Religions" and took stock of the ecumenical movement in the Catholic Church. An excerpt follows.

> Some persons think that the initial momentum of and enthusiasm toward ecumenism have waned. It is true that new difficulties have arisen within many individual churches, and those use up energy and diminish ecumenical efforts. It is not easy to work with others when our own house is not in good order.
>
> Meanwhile, the world itself is being drawn ever more rapidly, whether it wants to or not, into a vast network of intensifying relations across the globe. Inevitably Christians everywhere live and work more and more with Christians from churches other than their own and also with Muslims, Jews, Buddhists, Hindus and so on...
>
> Do these two opposing tendencies result in a threatening tension or can we discern the action of God's spirit here? There is an axiom in mental health work that tells us that the best way to free ourselves from preoccupation with our own interior struggles is to reach out in positive

> relationships with others. This broadens our horizons and tends to free us from self-occupation and the loss of a sense of proportion.
>
> The next thrust is already upon us: the need to build interfaith understanding and cooperation. This will be the most logical tool to combat secularism and materialism, as well as consumerism. Also it will be necessary to work together to clean up our atrocious environmental habits to salvage all forms of life on this planet, including human life itself.
>
> In the midst of all this, our ecumenical task shrinks back to size and can be approached with a more balanced perspective, a more integral point of view. Reaching out to other faiths may yet salvage our own Christian imperative of working for unity among ourselves. "For what seems to be God's foolishness is wiser than human wisdom, and what seems to be God's weakness is stronger than human strength" (1 Cor 1:25).

In the spring of 1992, Sister Libby was asked to be a board member of the Doane-Stuart school, an independent, co-ed ecumenical school formed when the Kenwood Academy, a school operated by the Religious of the Sacred Heart, merged with St. Agnes School, an Episcopal girls school.

In September of 1992, Sister Libby was awarded the Dr. Carlyle Adams Ecumenical Award from the Capital Area Council of Churches. Dr. S. Albert Newman, pastor of Westminster Presbyterian Church in Albany and president of the Capital Area Council of Churches, and Reverend James Kane, director of the Albany Roman Catholic Diocese Commission for Ecumenical and Interreligious Affairs, presented the award. Sister Libby was recognized for her efforts as a member of the Albany Diocesan Commission, her role as the Commission's representative on the Board of the Capital Area Council of Churches, and her Board membership at the Doane-Stuart School. The program for the award ceremony stated "In these various groups she has always tried to play an active role and to become a link—a bond—uniting people in Christ in spite of all human differences of opinion or difficulties of personality."

Sister Mary Gen played a key role in the establishment and development of the Ecumenical Baptism Witness Program in Albany in the early 1990s. As coordinator of the Program, Sister Mary Gen worked hard to recruit witnesses from different denominations as participants in this inter-denominational program. The program was a visible reminder that all baptisms are recognized in any Christian church and fostered inter-congregational connections in the diverse Christian churches in the Capital District. In 1998, Sister Mary Gen was also awarded the Carlyle Adams Ecumenical Award, primarily for her coordination of this program. Ian Leet, a member of the Reformed Church who was active in the Baptism Witness Program, remembers Sister Mary Gen as "very faithful about recruiting teams to witness the baptisms." In addition to her coordination of the Baptism Witness Program, in receiving the award, Sister Mary Gen was noted for her membership on the Board of the Capital District Council of Churches and the Roman Catholic Commission of Ecumenical and Interreligious Affairs of the Albany Diocese.

At least three Episcopal Bishops enjoyed evenings of relaxation with the Sisters at Abba House. Bishop Wilbur Hogg and Coajutor Daniel Herzog visited the House, individually for dinner and liturgy with the sisters, as well as with others for group events. Bishop David Ball recalls visiting the House several times a year for a number of years, where he would celebrate Mass in the living room and stay for dinner and conversation. He stated that he was always aware of its significance, both because it was a place of prayer and retreat, and because of its ecumenical nature.

Individuals from the same faith tradition as the Sisters benefited from exposure to the different faith traditions at Abba House. Anne Snyder considers herself "gifted with the ecumenical connections made there." Anne greatly enjoyed her numerous visits to Abba House, where she met many people from other faith traditions, and she believes that Abba House really moved her along on her "life journey to places where God intended [her] to go." When Sister Mary Gen left the Ecumenical Commission at the Diocese, Anne was asked to take her place. Anne also became active in an interfaith story circle.

Another friend of the House who appreciated the ecumenism was Justine Guernsey, a Catholic to Anglican convert who related to Sister Mary Gen's own conversion history. Justine said, "it was so good to be able to talk honestly with someone else who had done that." Justine found Abba House when she was in the process of discernment for the Episcopal Diaconate. Father Bob Limpert recommended she see Sister Libby for spiritual direction. She remembers that it was a natural choice for her to select Sister Libby be one of her presenters to the Anglican bishop when Justine was ordained as a deacon.

> *"They were strong but gentle women: very focused, with a clear sense of what they were doing."*
>
> *Deacon Justine Guernsey*

Interfaith Activities

Interfaith gathering at Abba House, circa 2000, with presenters of the Hindu faith. Sister Libby front left; directly behind her, Suhashini; behind her, Balu Dixit; to his right Balasubramanian, with his wife Rajalakshmi directly before him, Sister Mary Gen far right

> *"Sisters Libby and Mary Gen drew in a tapestry of people from all different faith traditions and wove them together into the fabric of Abba House."*
>
> *Walt Chura*

In the early 1990's, the Sisters' ecumenism made a natural shift outward to include faith traditions other than Christianity. According to Reverend Jim Kane, director of the Albany Roman Catholic Diocese Commission for Ecumenical an Interreligious Affairs, "Abba House was a wonderful beacon and mecca for ecumenical interfaith activities in the area. Long before ecumenism was 'popular,' Abba House was a highlight of ecumenical activities." In the 1980's, both Sister Libby and Sister Mary Gen were part of the Diocesan Commission for Ecumenical and Interreligious Affairs started by Howard Hubbard in 1968. They were also co-founding chair people of the Muslim Catholic dialogue.

> *"Libby and Mary Gen participate with enthusiasm in many ecumenical and interfaith groups and therefore we welcome persons of all faith in our home. Likewise we welcome opportunities to serve in other parishes or groups."*
>
> *September 1994*

From 1995 to 2000, the Sisters hosted annual interfaith events at Abba House with representatives from the local Hindu, Buddhist, Jewish, and Muslim communities. Bala (K. Balasubramanian) and his wife Raji were regular participants representing the Hindu community. Bala recalled that all of his memories of Abba House were very pleasant, and that he and his wife considered the Sisters friends, not simply connections in the interfaith community. While studying a photo taken at one of his presentations at the House, he commented, "*they* were the draw—those two women. Look at that smile!" he said, pointing to Sister Mary Gen. He also shared a copy of a letter written to him by Sister Libby after one of their presentations, which follows.

Nov. 21, 1995

Dear Good Friends,

Someday I will ask you about the correct way to address a married couple who are Hindu, but I can't wait to tell you our gratitude for the beautiful, informative and devotional evening you gave us last night! The people all were very pleased with your well-prepared and shared presentation, and we learned how much we have in common in spite of the obvious differences. For example, I remember scattering flower petals in a Eucharistic procession in church when I was a young girl. And the sharing of food that is also offered to God is another strong link. It is clearer and clearer that there is only one God behind all world religions.

Gratefully and affectionately,
Sister Libby Hoye

Bala noted that Sister Libby's letter was not a simple thank you, but a reflection: she had heard his presentation and reflected on it, identifying key parts of it with her own life experience, and then shared her connections with him. He remembers her ability to identify with others' experiences as one of the qualities that made her unique.

Early topics for the interfaith events included "Exploring the great riches found in other faith traditions" (1995) and "How to deal with problems in today's society" (1996). The Sisters looked for commonalities among the different faith traditions: the gathering in 1998 asked the questions: "How does your faith help you to become more loving to others?" and "How does your faith help you to endure the sufferings of life?" Sometimes the gatherings were used by the panelists to assess the condition of the different faith traditions, such as in 1999 when the topics were: "What is the state of each one's faith group in the Capital Area today and in the United States today?" and "How can we help one another?" The final interfaith gathering, held in 2001, was a fitting culmination of the years of interfaith work done by Abba House, titled simply "God and Morality: what we have in common."

Although not involved formally in the interfaith gatherings at Abba House, Rabbi Dan Ornstein's connection with Abba House was an example of how the Sisters lived out their openness to other faith traditions. According to Rabbi Dan, he was speaking with his friend Father Jim Kane in the late 1990s about a restlessness he was experiencing, saying that he felt as if he were "looking for something." Father Jim recommended that he try spiritual direction and referred him to Sister Libby at Abba House. Although Rabbi Dan met with Sister Libby for only a few months, he considered it a good introduction: he continued the practice with other directors for many years. He also led a few programs at the House that he enjoyed, one of which was a yearlong Bible study. Rabbi Dan liked the fact that Abba House was a retreat center located in the heart of an urban area. He lived in the same neighborhood as Abba House and would often drive by the House, see the sign and wonder about it. The Hebrew "Abba" drew him in, as a speaker of Hebrew. He also believed that the House contributed to the interfaith community: the fact that they attracted and welcomed a rabbi spoke to their openness. He said that the Sisters were quite grounded in their Catholic faith, which gave them the security to work with all people. After the Sisters left the House, he continued to visit when Sister Rosemary Sgroi was operating it as a spiritual life center, enjoying the peaceful atmosphere during his times of sabbatical.

> *"Sister Libby had a kind of open-hearted smile that was very welcoming."*
>
> *Rabbi Dan Ornstein*

Following is a Native American prayer used by the Sisters at an Abba House program in the late 1990's

> O GREAT SPIRIT,
> Whose voice I hear in the winds,
> And whose breath gives life to all the world,
> hear me! I am small and weak. I need your strength and wisdom.

> Let Me Walk in Beauty, and make my eyes
> ever behold the red and purple sunset.
> Make My Hands respect the things you have
> made and my ears sharp to hear your voice.
> Make Me Wise so that I may understand the
> things you have taught my people.
> Let Me Learn the lessons you have hidden
> in every leaf and rock.
> I Seek Strength, not to be greater than my
> brother, but to fight my greatest enemy—myself.
> Make Me Always Ready to come to you with
> clean hands and straight eyes.
> So When Life Fades, as the fading sunset,
> my spirit may come to you
> without shame.
>
> Princess Pale Moon, Ambassador of Friendship

The appreciation of other faith traditions exemplified by the Sisters of Abba House flowed from the rich prayer life of its founders. Sister Rose Marie Quilter spoke about it in Sister Libby's eulogy.

> Times of prolonged prayer and retreat at Mount Saviour, the Benedictine monastery in Elmira, New York, which became for Libby a true spiritual home, deepened and strengthened her prayer and led to a vigorous apostolate not only of hospitality to hundreds at Abba House every year, but in at least 14 specific commitments in the area of ecumenism, many of which she sustained for more than 10 years. She lists these among 'special events' for example, 'Participated in conference on Science and Faith of the Northeast Synod of the Presbyterian Church at Stony Point, New York. The committee in charge met monthly for a year at Abba House of Prayer.' Another excerpt: 'Sponsored, with Barry House, a public ecumenical dialogue—Experience of the Cross and Resurrection in the Work for Christian Unity.'

"May 'Abba,' the God of us all, bring you peace, pax, shalom, salaam, now and always."

Rev. James Kane, Abba House Memory Book 2001

My House—Growth Opportunities via Ego Deflation

We had a houseguest for a short time in 1997. My husband's uncle, who was 86 at the time, came from the Philippines to visit for about a week. He was a very strong-willed, traditional man with definite beliefs. He had survived the Bataan Death March during WWII, an event that must have impacted his character. My husband was a young boy during the Japanese occupation in the Philippines, and he occasionally speaks about different events from that time, usually noting that Americans, in general, take too much for granted.

"The Uncle" was quite tolerant of our five-year-old son when he barged into the guest room or stepped on his feet. He also had positive exchanges with our older son, who always managed to behave well for the short periods when we had guests, probably in part because attention was diverted away from him. The Uncle and I had some difficulty communicating, at least from my perspective. I attempted to engage him in conversation, but most of the time he appeared to be ignoring my comments, although when I spoke he would glance in my general direction, look somewhere over the top of my head and talk toward the topic of conversation without personally addressing me. The only time I recall challenging him was when he told our younger son that boys do not cry.

I attempted to focus on the benefits of his visit. I learned more about my husband by listening to him converse with the Uncle. He was also an interesting person who told fascinating stories, and there was more peace in the house than we had experienced in a long time because no one was yelling. And the visit was not open-ended: there was a set departure date, since the Uncle had an itinerary with several more legs to his journey to complete before returning to the Philippines.

Mornings, the Uncle, an early riser, would already be sitting at the kitchen table having his breakfast when I entered, prior to my early morning quiet time with my Bible. Since I had already discovered the value of daily prayer, nothing and no one kept me from it. While the Uncle was with us, I would pour my coffee and go quietly into the other room to pray and read the Scriptures. He would nod. In my prayer journal I wrote about the visit.

> At first I felt irritated and intruded upon, but then I prayed more. This past Sunday morning one of my readings said that I should always seek to understand others and then I will love them more. Since then I have noticed what an inquisitive mind the Uncle has! He is always interested in learning new things, which is pretty amazing in a man of his age. And he is very tolerant of the children.
>
> I realize how God's grace has been poured into me this past week. I have been blessed with more tolerance than I thought I could ever demonstrate. In the past I would have been very upset by this judgmental, opinionated man. I truly believe this ability to try to see beneath the bluster is a gift from God. I could never reach inside myself and pull out such riches unless God had placed them there. This morning prayer time is essential to my walk with God: each day I am blessed to have the wisdom to keep doing it. Sometimes I do it blindly, in faith, and sometimes I run here in desperation. But I show up, each day. Thank you, God!

I continued to follow Sister Libby's advice to "keep showing up."

The day before the Uncle was scheduled to leave, he approached me in the morning when I was getting my coffee. He had a book in his hand called The Book of God which he had found on the shelves of my spiritual library. The book was an attempt to make the Bible into a narrative account in order to increase its readability. The Uncle showed me the book, told me that he had been reading a few passages and was enjoying it. He said he had trouble reading the Bible, but found this book easy to read. He said, "I am enlightened." I was quite moved. Naturally, I told him to keep the book, and to take it with him. He was very grateful.

On the day he was scheduled to leave, I went into the kitchen where he was sitting to say goodbye and wish him a safe trip. He stood up and said, "I want to give you a blessing." I don't remember what the blessing was, but I do remember the feel of his hand on my head as he prayed for me. I was deeply touched and thanked him before I kissed him on the cheek and left the house.

> I wrote in my journal:
>
> God always surprises me. God's children always surprise me, too. I saw that God uses the most unexpected people, times and situations to speak to us. He used my husband's uncle to bless me. I felt the wash of the Holy Spirit move over me when the Uncle put his hand on my head, and I was blessed and prayed for. I am very grateful that I did not reject this gift by a show of pride on my part, which I could easily have done. This was such a clear 'blessing' from God—usually His blessings are quite a bit subtler than this one. If I pay attention, I can see that God is speaking to me every single minute of every day.

God was (and still is) working on my ego. I don't enjoy that, but I understand it is part of my spiritual growth. A few years later, when I was in a a Bible-based weight loss program, I heard someone refer to herself as "fleshly." That annoyed me somehow—reminded me of saints and martyrs wearing hair shirts to punish themselves for sins that only they could identify. But I can see how "sins" or "character defects" or tendencies to be "fleshly" are connected to my ego: I usually enjoy doing the things that often lead to pain, like overeating, smoking, gossiping, excessive television-watching. Most of my self-destructive tendencies are the result of fear and self-centeredness, which God continues to help me identify. I am grateful to Him, but often annoyed (you can be like that with someone who loves you). Every time I start to feel a little smug or self-righteous about my progress, I either run into someone who reminds me where I have come from or am disturbed by old feelings that I thought I had let go of. For me, spiritual growth is usually slow and sometimes achingly painful.

Adding to my emotional confusion during this time in my life were the hormone treatments I was undergoing for endometriosis. I wrote in my journal:

> Things are just so screwy. I am definitely not myself. I am very emotional, weepy and easily disturbed. I pray, but the words don't seem to reach my heart. My husband and I argue. Things that didn't bother me before seem huge and looming. I am afraid of the future. I am miserable in the present. I have migraine headaches. I have pain in my legs. I am gaining weight.
>
> Oh Lord, can you help me please? Can you show me a little of what is happening? Can you spare a little peace, some serenity for your servant? I feel like I am not doing your will, either. I feel like I'm alone by the side of the road. Help me to remember that pain is the touchstone of spiritual growth. Thank you for hearing me, for always seeing me. I will try to keep joy and gratitude in my day today.

It was the praise at the end that kept me going. I was learning to praise even in the storms.

I realized through my daily prayer time that the strong mood swings I was experiencing as a result of the medical treatment were a blessing in a strange way. I was deeply feeling both the "lows" and the "highs" in my life. Interesting, my older son was experiencing his own emotional extremes, so perhaps this experience increased my empathy for him. When I was sad I was incredibly sad, but when I was happy I was truly joy-filled. I remembered feeling similar to that when I was in college. It seemed like I was recapturing something I had lost. It was different to feel so intensely and not want to escape from it in some way. I was learning to feel my feelings without fear.

My 38th birthday in early September brought some major changes. On the day itself, we filed a PINS (Persons in Need of Supervision) report against our older son, on the advice of several of the professionals we had been working with. I felt tired and hopeless as we filed the paperwork. I didn't think it would make any difference in his behavior (it didn't), and I found venturing into the legal system was discouraging. I just never thought we would have to go down that road. He had always been a basically good kid—got into a few scrapes, but we could reason with him—until he turned eleven. And he still showed moments of great sensitivity, such as he exhibited when he gave me my birthday gift that year. He had bought it at one of our favorite stores in Hampton Beach, New Hampshire, where we vacationed as a family every summer. Knowing that I sat and read my Bible for prayer time each morning, he had bought me a lovely, small, tabletop wooden plaque with a crucifix and a votive light. I was deeply moved by the gift. The moments like this when he showed his thoughtful side were the ones that I remembered and held onto during tough times in the years to come. Even now, I continue to light a candle in that votive holder almost every morning when I sit down to pray.

That same September, Sister Libby asked me to be a member of the Abba House Board of Directors. Finally I felt like I had "arrived." In retrospect, I can see that the sisters chose the Board members based on their knowledge of the members' spirituality, gifts and talents, prayerfully considering how each person would complement the mission and goals of the House. Through the years I found that being a member of the Board at Abba House was spiritually and personally enriching. Through my Board tenure, I met many wonderful people who touched my life in countless ways. And by sitting on that Board at regular meetings, I learned how to listen and pay attention while in a group of diverse individuals, and I learned how to take the temperature of the room when there were a variety of personalities present. That ability to observe and contribute has served me well in both my professional and personal life.

ABBA HOUSE—ROOTS OF THE RELIGIOUS OF THE SACRED HEART

"Sister Libby and Sister Mary Gen brought the RSCJ professionalism to everything they did."
Patricia Crewel

The founders of Abba House of Prayer were members of the Society of the Sacred Heart, a group of women Religious that was established by Madeleine Sophie Barat, who was born in Joigny, France in 1779 and canonized a Saint in 1925. Madeleine Sophie, as she was called during her lifetime, was born into the turbulent times of the French Revolution when a person's very survival depended upon political affiliations. That was also the age of enlightenment, when people were encouraged to think for themselves rather than to follow societal institutions, like the Roman Catholic church. As in most areas of the world at the time, women were viewed as inferior to men and had few rights or privileges in French society.

In the midst of this environment, Madeleine Sophie Barat emerged as a leader, establishing a new religious congregation of women that would eventually grow into an international community that included over 3000 women by the time of her death in 1865. She was elected Superior General for Life in 1806 at the young age of twenty-seven, although her leadership of the early community started informally when she was barely twenty. The

Society was formulated with the help of Father Joseph Varin, a contemporary of Sophie Barat's priest brother Louis.

> Following are St. Madeleine Sophie's words describing her vision for the Society.
>
> The primordial idea of our little Society of the Sacred Heart was to gather together young girls to establish a community, which night and day would adore the Heart of Jesus outraged in his Eucharistic love. But, I said, when we shall be twenty-four religious able to replace each other on the prie-dieu to keep up perpetual adoration, that will be much but very little to do for so noble an end. But if we had pupils whom we could form to the spirit of adoration, how different that would be! And I saw those hundreds, those thousands of adorers as an ideal and universal ostensorium lifted above the Church...We shall raise up a throng of adorers from all nations and to the very ends of the earth.
>
> Happy Memories of A Saint
> (Les Loisirs de l'Abbaye) P. Perdreau, p. 422

Madeleine Sophie remained true to that vision throughout her entire life.

The nineteenth century was a fruitful time for new religious communities in France: between 1800 and 1820 a total of thirty-five communities of women were founded in that country and that momentum continued with an average of six new communities starting each year between 1820 and 1880. Among the communities founded at that time that remain vital today are the Little Sisters of the Poor (LSP—1839), the Religious of the Sacred Heart of Mary (RSHM—1849), and the Congregation of Our Lady of the Cenacle (RC—1843). Each community had its area of specialization in the renewal of France, which had been devastated by events surrounding the French Revolution.

Madeleine Sophie had been provided with an unusually extensive education for a young woman, through the efforts of her brother Louis, who was eleven years her senior, as well as her godfather and a priest. It was not surprising that she found her calling as a provider of education for young women. The Society of the Sacred Heart established schools for the young women of France: both girls from the wealthier families in boarding schools, and girls from the poorer families in day schools. As new "houses" sprung up during the years the Society grew, the schools dedicated to these two different groups of female students were usually located on the same property.

Madeleine Sophie Barat believed strongly that her community should be centered on discovering and communicating the love of the Sacred Heart of Jesus, with its members devoted to living lives of both prayer and service. For years, the Society was known as a contemplative congregation with some action in the sphere of education and a prayer life similar to the Carmelites, a religious order founded in the twelfth century, who trace their roots to a group of hermits with a sincere devotion to the Blessed Mother of Jesus. The changes resulting from the Second Vatican Council Members led to the Society of the Sacred Heart's change in classification from a contemplative to an educational congregation. RSCJ's have always been encouraged to develop a strong interior spirit—a sense of prayerfulness—combined with a deep humility attained through oneness with the hearts of Jesus and His mother Mary. That charism has remained the wellspring of the Society for over two hundred years.

> *"What was the distinguishing feature of the first Noviceship in the Society...? Just one thing...one single basic virtue... essential to every religious of the Sacred Heart, a virtue that is both unique and all-powerful: an interior spirit."*
> An Interior Spirit, *Saint Madeleine Sophie Barat, p. 9.*

The ministry of Abba House of Prayer seems a natural outcropping from the deep interior prayer life of the members of the Society combined with their calling to educate. Mother Barat once told the novices about her interpretation of the Easter dawn meeting between Mary Magdalene and Christ:

> There is the spirit of the Society. Our first movement is to linger at the feet of the Master; that is the contemplative life, that is what we must do in prayer. But it is then that Jesus says to us: "Go, tell my brothers." Mary becomes

> an apostle. Why can we not say to the whole universe: "Know his Heart?"
>
> The Society of the Sacred Heart: History of a Spirit,
> Margaret Williams, RSCJ, p. 302

Mother Barat saw this precious, prayerful balance between contemplation and action as a commonality between the Society of the Sacred Heart and Jesuit spirituality. She also identified greatly with the Carmelite standard of deep contemplative prayer. She spoke of these at a conference of the Society in 1835.

> In the century of Saint Teresa the Church had need of two orders, one which would offer to God fervent prayer to move him and obtain the salvation of men [people], and another which would combat valiantly under the standard of Jesus Christ. . . One was the order of the reformed Carmel, the other the Company of Jesus formed by the companions of Saint Ignatius. One was like Moses praying on the mountain, the other like Aaron fighting on the plain. And they both had great need of prayer, as their founders recognized so well. Our Society which is made for both these works—the practice of prayer and the salvation of men—must draw its strength from contemplation.
>
> The Society of the Sacred Heart: History of a Spirit,
> Margaret Williams, RSCJ, p. 306

Contemporaries of the Abba House Sisters

In an effort to interview some of the contemporaries of Sisters Libby and Mary Gen who were members of the congregation during the time they established Abba House, in 2009 I visited Teresian House, a retirement center in Albany where several of the sisters were living. Sister Mary Parkinson, an early member of the Abba Community in the early 1970's, showed me a photo of herself, Rose Marie, Mary Gen, Libby & Mabel Dorsey from 1971. Sister Mary remembers that Sister Libby was a "good soul," and that "she didn't have it too easy, poor dear." Abba House started at a time when the status quo was changing in the church, and as a result, there were major changes within both religious communities and the laity. She said that Sister Libby "wasn't doing anything to separate them [RSCJ], but was trying to keep them going." This was an allusion to some of the difficulties that Sister Libby encountered in attempting to start and to operate a House of Prayer. Sister Mary also remembered meeting Brother David Steindl-Rast on a trip to Mount Saviour.

Sister Gertrude Cosenke said that she enjoyed going to Abba House because they were very welcoming and "I felt like I was among my own, since we were all RSCJ's." Sister Gertrude, who worked as a director of religious education at a parish in the South End in Albany for over 25 years, was at Maria College at the same time Sister Libby attended nursing school. She said that Libby already had several degrees: "She could have taught many of the classes there." Libby told her that, during the commencement ceremony, as Bishop Broderick shook her hand, he said to her "oh, are ***you*** here?" Prior to the beginning of Abba House, Sister Gertrude lived at the Academy of the Sacred Heart in New York City, across from Central Park, when Libby was the sacristan there and also taught Science. Sister Gertrude's quote from the Memory Book follows.

> When Abba Community was moving from Kenwood to Western Avenue, Libby Hoye was also studying at Maria College for her RN. It was a very demanding time for her and I admired her courage. I know Libby and Mary Gen were a wonderful team. Their contribution to the Diocese in Faith Formation and Spirituality was tremendous.

Sister Frances Murphy said that she went to some lectures at Abba House. She was humbly clear about what she felt her role was there, saying that she supported them with her presence—that was how she helped out. She contributed the following to the Memory Book.

> Sisters Libby Hoye and Mary Gen Smyth have given much to the diocese and generously opened their house to various ecumenical events with excellent speakers. For

> their work, I am sure, they are much appreciated. We wish Mary Gen the best in her new work, and are happy to have Libby with us at Kenwood.

Sister Cora McLaughlin, also in residence at Teresian House, said I could use her quote from the Memory Book: "Great admiration for the courage of these two who 'sailed out' on a venture for the church in Albany." Sister Grail McMullen, also at Kenwood along with her sister, Faine McMullen, contributed the following to the Memory Book.

> Shortly after our arrival at Kenwood . . . Faine and I began to attend some of the stimulating and helpful events held at Abba House: days of recollections, lectures, Bible study classes and interfaith meetings. The anniversary celebration with Father Raymond Brown [SS] was a glorious event.

My House—Crisis Point

This kind can only come out through prayer.
Mark 9:29

In mid-September of 1997, I awoke one morning with flu-like symptoms, and was quite sick for a week. This was the first of many times when I would be "felled" by some mysterious illness that immobilized me for days, keeping me in my house and away from my various volunteer activities. Before I got ill this time, my good friend Irene told me that she was worried about me because I was "doing too much." She said, "I'm afraid you're not setting a good example for your boys—that we have to do good works in order to be worthy." I'm sure she knew that I was more likely to hear her concern if she framed it around my children, who were the center of my world. So, I decided to reevaluate my commitments and try to find more balance between home, work and community/church activities.

In early October, I stole away to Abba House for a few days. The sisters were in and out so I had some time alone in the House. It really did feel like home as I fixed my dinner, read at table, listened to music in the living room, and helped a little bit by doing some laundry in the basement. When Sister Libby was there we talked a few times. She told me that it was time for me to take care of myself, and that there would be plenty of time for me to take care of others in the future. She said I would always be doing some of that because it was in my nature. She knew me.

And I knew her, too. As much as I loved Sister Libby, I disagreed with her at times, particularly about my son: as he got sicker, she began to suggest more often that he be institutionalized. Actually, we were beginning to investigate temporary residential treatment options, primarily because it seemed more and more that he needed constant care and boundaries, but I never considered institutionalization. I also found some of her suggestions for advancing my spiritual life unrealistic, given our family circumstances. For example, she suggested one half hour of silence in the house at night with all electronics turned off, in an effort to help me carve out my quiet time. I knew I didn't have the strength to make that happen. Every time we attempted to instill structure or boundaries in our house it seemed to result in a battle with our older son; I had to choose my battles wisely in an attempt to conserve my energy and keep us safe, as my son could become verbally or physically abusive if we interrupted him during an activity he was involved with. But Sister Libby was also a realist. She had been the first person to put to words the possibility that my son had a mental illness. Coming to terms with that expression and that reality was challenging for me.

Peaceful moments at home became rare in the next few months, as my journal reminds me:

> I pray to God and all the angels, saints and anyone else who will listen to help me and my family today. Sometimes all of this is so difficult and I get very tired and sad. I pray for strength and wisdom and love and patience and hope. I know that God has not carried us this far to drop us at this vulnerable point in our lives.

And a few days later:

> O God I believe. Help thou my unbelief. I want to trust you, but everything is clamoring at me. My child defies me, is physical, insulting, annoying, refusing to do his schoolwork or anything else. His teachers call and complain. What am I to do? Nothing? Pray? Trust in you as I watch everything fall apart? If I were a better mother

> would this not be happening? Please help me get through this horrible time in our lives!

And, as God so often does, when I cried out loudly enough, He sent help. Within a month, after numerous calls and meetings at home and school, we checked our son into a psychiatric hospital because he was "in crisis." He finally met the criteria for in-patient treatment: he wanted to "harm himself or others." That was when things got really raw and scary, but God was right there in the trenches with us through it all.

****

My son's caseworker made a joke that came to represent the many years of dealing with his illness.

> During his prayer time, a man cried out to God for the desires of his heart. He heard God say, "my son, my ways are not your ways. To me a thousand years are like a minute and a million dollars are like a penny." The man said, "God, can I have a penny?" God answered "in a minute."

Now I smile every time I read or hear a Bible verse about God and time because I know He was definitely speaking to me with that joke. My son's recovery from these deadly illnesses was not to be in my time, it was to be in God's time. And that—in my experience—can most certainly take a long time.

But that was such a surreal time.

Thanksgiving at the hospital: I stayed for the day because I couldn't bear the thought of him being without family on Thanksgiving. We got our orange plastic cafeteria trays and stood in line for our turkey and potatoes and gravy and corn. Most of the kids on the adolescent unit had at least one family member with each of them, so there was quite a bit of laughter and affection, which was nice. Still, I felt my heart in my throat. We had soft ice cream for dessert. That made it easier for me to swallow. I kept looking around and thinking, "I can't believe we are here."

I prayed so hard. At work I kept a prayer on my desk that was attributed to Julian of Norwich, and I read it over and over during the day. It gave me great comfort then and still does today: "All shall be well, and all shall be well, and all manner of thing shall be well, and in this God wishes us to be enclosed in rest and in peace." I clung to that prayer, believing that someday my son would be well again.

When one of his many doctors told me it was possible he would have to stay in a hospital-type setting forever because he might never get better, I cried out to God for mercy and help. Sometimes I screamed in my car at the top of my lungs because I was so angry, frustrated and frightened. But God has broad shoulders. He could handle my fits. And the screaming helped me feel better. Within a day or two someone new would come along to help. Or I would be given a beautiful prayer experience.

In the area of my prayer life, it seemed like God was rewarding me for my continuing efforts to progress. I met regularly with Sister Libby for spiritual direction and found our sessions to be encouraging, for the most part. She gave me a variety of suggestions for deepening and enriching my prayer time, many of which I was able to use. I also felt good about myself in this area because I was taking tangible steps toward improving this part of my life. I was encouraged, and so I persevered, and reaped many benefits from my time with God. Sometimes I felt as if I were falling in love. I remember special times like driving in my car alone and being moved to tears by a love song on the radio that described my feelings. Or going to noon Mass at Cathedral and spending the entire time just staring at my arm and thinking "Jesus had an arm like mine. God had an arm like mine." If you really think about it, it's a pretty awesome connection that we are all made in the image and likeness of our creator.

The day-to-day reality of going to work, being a wife and mother to the family remaining at home and driving back and forth to the hospital for therapy sessions, visits and meetings with the doctors was very tiring. I wrote in my prayer journal:

> I need to remain teachable through this process. Sometimes I can feel myself closing down, shutting the door of my heart and mind. Last night we went to group

at the hospital. I should be grateful, but I'm exhausted. I should be joyful, but I'm sad. I should feel supported, but I feel numb. There is so much at stake here.

God, please help me to stay open and teachable. Holy Spirit, open my eyes and calm my mind. Jesus, please walk with me through this minefield. I know my son is in the right place. Now I have to deal with his being there. I don't know how to handle that.

Today I will remember Psalm 72—He shall be like rain coming down on the meadow. My soul needs refreshment.

Daily prayer and meditation became my time of refreshment, when I desperately needed sustenance. God became my lifeline. I would sit with my Bible, prayer journal, and whatever other books I was using during daily prayer and rise up thirty to sixty minutes later energized and encouraged. On the days when I could quiet my mind, I practiced Centering Prayer, and was even more refreshed.

The professional help we received as a family allowed us to communicate some of our deeper fears and feelings with each other, including our love. My husband was incredibly supportive at this time: he was a rock for all of us. When one of the doctors told us that our son's illness could be genetic and untreatable, he refused to repeat it or believe it. He took on the role of bringing our son to weekly therapy at the hospital after the discharge in early December. And so we crept toward the holidays, cautiously and slowly.

****

It was a bittersweet Christmas, nice to have the family back together, but so difficult with all the extenuating circumstances of my physical pain and our son's illness. I tried to do all the things I usually did to make the holidays happy and memorable, but I was in nearly constant endometrial pain. I had gained ten pounds with my hormone treatments, with little pain relief. Our younger son got the flu and was very sick for four days, which I nursed him through. It was looking like he would need to have his tonsils removed due to repeated bouts of tonsillitis. And we were all walking on eggshells, wondering when our older son's next breakdown would come. It didn't take long.

Within a few weeks, we were at a crisis point again: dangerous violence in our home. An entry from my prayer journal follows.

> God's ways are certainly not my ways! If this is His idea of a plan, then my mortal ignorance is confirmed with each new twist, because I am baffled! I cannot think of a reason why we should all be going through this!

I was angry because I knew we were unsafe in our home and the local hospital did not deem our son a danger to us or to himself. A few weeks later, more violence led to him once again being removed from the house. This time he was hospitalized, and based on their observations, he was not returned to our home. He was placed in an interim shelter awaiting placement, a short-term arrangement that stretched out into several months while we worked with the court system and professionals to find a facility that would meet his needs.

I retreated to the sanctuary of Abba House whenever I could, cloistering myself in one of the guest rooms upstairs with my journal, Bible, and the books from their library. In February of 1998, I started a new journal while on retreat at the house, preparing myself emotionally and spiritually for the process of sending my son to a residential treatment facility. There I worked through my feelings of inadequacy as a mother, confusion about how to communicate our family situation with my adult stepchildren and their families, and my sadness and grief. I wrote and cried and prayed and slept, all things I needed to do in order to keep my own sanity and remain functional.

Gains in rest and peace of mind were short-lived: an entry from my journal less than two weeks after that retreat follows.

> Oh God, I am so weary. I feel fire-tried and tested, worn out beyond endurance. I do not know how much more of

> this I can endure. I cry at you, I shake my fist and ask why? I will be so valuable once I get out of this crucible: what would you have me do? It must be something important to you. I know that your ways are not my ways, but I am only human, Lord. I am exhausted. Help me to get some rest please.

That's the way it was in my house during those years: it seemed that we were either tense or more tense, but never very peaceful for very long.

Abba House—Bible Studies

The Bible was definitely one of the cornerstones of life at Abba House. Both sisters had a great love of and familiarity with Scripture that they credited largely to their novice director at Kenwood, Marie Louise Schroen, RSCJ, who used the Bible more than any other text during their novitiate. At Abba House it was rare to pray without using Scripture, so the Sisters' prayer lives were just as full of the Word as their Bible studies.

The Abba House Sisters lived out their RSCJ charism as educators by teaching Bible studies throughout their thirty-year ministry. Over the years, the sisters offered a total of nearly eighty series of Bible classes, many of them outside Abba House. Both sisters taught Bible classes at a number of Roman Catholic parishes in the Albany Diocese, including St. Paul the Apostle in Schenectady, St. Madeleine Sophie and Christ the King in Guilderland, St. Margaret Mary in Albany, St. Adalbert in Schenectady, St. John's in Rensselaer and several other parishes.

All of the classes were taught by either Sister Libby or Sister Mary Gen, and met weekly from September through May, with some weeks off during the year for holidays. This expanse of time allowed for rich exploration of a particular book of the Bible that the sisters moved through chronologically, providing deep discussion and reflection. Sometimes, the Sisters taught on a theme that ran through several books of the Bible, such as compassion, prophets/mystics, faith, women in Scripture, and the Holy Spirit. Both sisters were gifted at raising the consciousness of their students on issues of peace, justice and non-violence within the context of their Bible classes, other program offerings and in their daily lives.

Sister Libby and Sister Mary Gen taught two formal weekly classes at Abba House from the mid 1970's through their departure in 2001, usually one during the day and one in the evening, on different days of the week. Anyone who attended these classes would agree with a statement from the Sisters' 1997 program letter: "Fellowship flows abundantly in both these groups each year as we grow in the Lord together."

The sisters prepared mindfully for the Bible classes they taught. In their September 3, 1985 Letter to Friends, they announced the Bible topics for the year: "The topic will be the Old Testament books of Samuel and of Kings and we have been buying books and researching these topics with keen interest." They drew upon the insights and knowledge gained during their personal trips to the Holy Land. Sister Mary Gen was a gifted photographer and she incorporated many of the slides she took from her several trips there into her Bible study classes. Sister Libby enrolled in courses each summer at the Boston College Institute of Religious Education and Pastoral Ministry, which greatly enhanced her teaching.

Betty Ann Hart was friend of Abba House who regularly attended Bible study classes for many years. Through her attendance and participation in the classes at Abba House, she became quite comfortable with reading the Bible. She liked the way the sisters made the attendees use their Bibles during classes to look up Scripture. This practice made her better able to read and study the Scriptures on her own. Betty Ann also commented that the Sisters encouraged everyone to think independently, and to draw their own conclusions as they read and studied the Scriptures.

The Sisters enjoyed familiarizing lay people with the Bible. A February 22, 1996 article in the Evangelist titled "Catholics can study Bible as part of Lenten exercises" featured plenty of "pointers" from the Abba House sisters. They encouraged people who wanted to commit to reading the Bible during Lent to find a scholarly but easily readable translation, making sure that it had good footnotes. Although Bible commentaries were mentioned as a resource for education, the sisters encouraged people to join a Bible class such as the ones offered at Abba House and other parishes. They noted that the Bible is an entire library of books by different authors that encompasses more than 3,000 years of history. As such, it takes time to become familiar with it and to know it well. The article emphasized that God speaks to the reader through the Bible, and it is important to take time to listen to God after reading, realizing that God's messages often come gradually through the day after a time of Scripture study early on. Sister Mary Gen was quoted, "You could be having a very good prayer in the morning, and it isn't until the afternoon when you're washing the dishes that God speaks to you."

The article also contained the following list of "Do's" and "Don'ts" for people studying Scripture during Lent. The "do and don't" format doesn't quite fit with the hallmark openness exhibited by Abba House through its 30 year ministry, but it summarizes many of their often expressed beliefs regarding Scripture study.

DO

- **Get comfortable.** "It's alright to be comfortable," Sister Mary Gen said. Many people like to set aside a "sacred space" in their homes, where they can sit in a comfortable chair, away from noise and interruptions, and read the Bible and pray in the morning or evening.
- **Say a prayer to the Holy Spirit** before you begin your daily reading, asking for inspiration to see the connections between Scripture and your own life.
- **Choose a single book to focus on** and read it in depth, rather than trying to read a set number of pages each day.
- **Go further when you're ready** with other books or resources, study groups, courses or spiritual direction.

DON'T

- **Don't try to read the entire Bible all the way through.** Unless you're "well-educated in some other field" the nuns said you're bound to be overwhelmed and confused. "The Bible is not meant to be read like a novel."
- **Don't read only the Sunday Mass readings.** The Church has "a great system" of including an Old Testament reading, psalm, New Testament reading and Gospel passage at Mass, Sister Libby said, but "each is just a snippet

of a whole book." It's better to read one entire book than brief passages from several.

- **Don't give up.** There are dozens of study groups, guided companions and resources available for anyone interested in learning about the Bible.

Although the Bible Study classes were offered weekly throughout the year and people were encouraged to attend regularly, the sisters understood that many people had commitments that prevented them from attending regularly. Sister Mary Gen was quoted in a September 15, 1988 Evangelist article about Abba House, "There is a somewhat linear structure to the classes, but people should feel free to attend even if they have to miss a few of the sessions." Sister Libby added, "We realize that lay people with busy lives can't be academic about it. This is not so much an academic background as it is taking the Scripture and seeing how it relates to your life."

The Bible was indeed a cornerstone of life at Abba House. Both sisters were very aware of global trends and Gospel responses, and mindfully and effectively brought the two worlds together. Rose Marie Quilter, RSCJ, one of the first five members of the original Abba Community, aptly described the role the Bible played in their daily life: "His Word then becomes the standard of our lives: it rebukes, strengthens, cleanses, heals, nourishes us. He, the Word of God, makes us a community."

Here is a sampling of the books of Scripture the Sisters taught during their thirty-year ministry. It is only a partial list: the complete list is far longer.

1976-77	Gospel of John
1978-79	Gospels of John and Luke
1979-80	Book of Wisdom, Acts of the Apostles, Genesis/Exodus
1985-86	Old Testament Books of Samuel and Kings
1987-88	Book of Exodus
1988-89	Letters of St. Paul
1990-91	Gospel of John

1991-92	The Books of Wisdom, Themes in the Gospel of John
1994-95	Progressive revelation of the Holy Spirit from Genesis through Revelation
1997-98	Gospel of Mark w/ preliminary instruction on the Bible itself & how to read it. Prophets and Mystics of modern times and in the Bible itself and how they relate.
1998-99	Gospel of John, Acts of the Apostles

Along with their love of Scripture, the Sisters had a great love of the Holy Land. Father Paul Roman led many pilgrimages to Italy, Jerusalem and other spiritual places over the years, and he brought one or the other of the Abba House sisters on several of them. He told me about one trip to the Tomb of Saint Peter where he was saying Mass with about thirty individuals who had accompanied him on the trip. Father Roman had brought along copies of the *Magnificat*, a Roman Catholic Mass guide, for everyone to use, since it was also a spiritual retreat. Earlier in the day they had planned the liturgy they were going to have at the Tomb of St. Peter, with the readings and prayers divided up between the participants. During the Consecration, Father Roman said that he was sometimes blessed with the ability to see the face of Jesus on the host when he elevated it, and that this occurred during the Mass at St. Peter's Tomb. He said that his demeanor must have indicated that he saw something, because afterward Sister Libby asked him what had happened at that time. He explained what he had seen, stating that it was something that happened to him occasionally. The next day when he said Mass for the group again, Sister Libby told him after the Mass that she had also seen the face of Jesus on the host.

> *"She was very spiritual" Father Roman said about Sister Libby.*

Sister Mary Gen received a study grant from the RSCJ's to go abroad to Israel, Egypt and Greece and study both the Bible and the biblical sites in those countries. The trip lasted three months and was part of an international program from the Catholic Theological Union in Chicago.

(See Programs section for examples of Scripture based programs.)

> *"We feel blessed and privileged to have this lifestyle and ministry and expect to continue as long as God provides the strength and the where-with-all. Most of you have greatly helped Him to do this over the years. Thank you again!"*
>
> *From September 1991 Letter to Friends*

My House—Changes & Choices

During the two years before he was removed from our home, our older son stopped believing in God. He had been a spiritual child who related easily to God, but at eleven he started resisting. I suppose he felt like God had deserted him. He put all the items from his room having to do with religion or spirituality in a box in the spare room. That box frightened me.

However, I knew that we were protected on some level. One morning, before our son was removed from our house, when I opened my eyes, I saw someone standing near my bed. He was facing me, but was not looking at me. Instead, he was staring straight ahead resolutely, in the direction of my son's bedroom. He had something that looked like a feathered breastplate on his chest. He was beautiful. I closed my eyes and saw his outline etched in gold behind my eyelids. When I opened my eyes again he was gone. Months later I was looking at a book of angels in my church's religious education office and found pictures of a man that looked like him. I believe he was a warrior angel (I like to think he was Michael) sent to protect my family.

It certainly felt like there was evil in the house. I didn't understand it but I felt it. When my son left our house, a lightness entered. And the exit was good for him as well. In March, still at the shelter, my son told me that he had started to pray again, which I found comforting. All it takes is for the door to open a tiny crack for God to enter in. The door was starting to open for my son.

I prayed for faith and was rewarded. I told my son and others that he would be well again. I believed that someday he would be self-supporting. I became his greatest advocate. But I was going through my own health difficulties, as my endometriosis continued to be painful. When I occasionally re-read my prayer journal, I could see how I would pray for help and a few weeks later my prayers would be answered. For example, in mid-March, I wrote about the intense physical pain I was having, as well as my low self-esteem around my inability to stop overeating and smoking. I wrote: "Please help me to feel better about myself so I can do your work today." Two weeks later I wrote about starting treatment with a pain management specialist for my endometriosis, which got me through the next few months.

At this time, I was also beginning to really dislike my job. I was blessed with good pay and able to do a lot of varied work like writing and training, but I felt like it wasn't enough. I thought I wasn't "making a difference" in the world and that I should be doing something more important. I felt unfulfilled and miserable. I was working on my spiritual life and trying to become less self-centered, but I was clearly very self-centered at work. Because of my deeper spiritual walk and the work I was doing on my own character defects, it bothered me when I acted in an un-loving manner at work. When a stressful situation occurred, such as a re-organization or a staffing change in my office, I would revert to old coping mechanisms. For example, to make myself feel better about my own actions, I would focus on other people's mistakes and gossip with my co-workers about them. I would return sarcasm from touchy co-workers with my own sarcastic comments, turning negativity and criticism into a sort of bantering humor in order to lessen the sting. I would come home at night exhausted by my own misbehavior and complain mightily to my poor husband, who worked in the same unit but was somehow able to avoid internalizing the negativity in the workplace.

Praying and talking to friends and family about my dissatisfaction in my career led me to look at the times in my life when I felt happiest. It was very noticeable that my abdominal pain nearly disappeared whenever I was teaching religious education. I began to see this as a sign from God that I should be serving him through my church, so I started exploring possibilities for a new career in that area. After some research, I discovered that, not only are most lay positions in my church woefully underpaid, many of them also require advanced academic degrees. So I would have to make great investments of time and money, with nominal financial returns for my investment. That didn't seem wise, especially since I was considering leaving an extremely stable position in state government where I was well paid, respected, and received excellent benefits.

So I took another look. I noticed that the pain also went away when I was training at work. Maybe I should look into teaching! I remembered the comment Sister Libby had made the year before to the woman in her scripture study class: "Listen to Anne, she is an educator!" I thought about the time I spent with my younger son, playing letter and color Bingo with him (complete with nifty, inexpensive prizes). I pondered earlier times before my older son stopped being interested in academics when I was able to help him with his homework. I thought about how much I loved the children in my religious education classes and the thoughtful gifts they gave me, particularly the little crystal "teacher angel" that I cherished from one of my girls. I began seriously considering the possibility of changing careers and becoming a teacher.

At the same time, more rich and beautiful spiritual experiences were happening. Through my time at Abba House, I was becoming more comfortable with imaginative prayer. During difficult periods, I would imagine Jesus taking my hand and leading me, or sitting in the car and talking to me while I drove, or walking in the park with me. This ability to see Jesus in my mind's eye and to feel His presence with me allowed me to tap into a deeper spiritual level. From my journal:

> Today I picture myself taking Jesus' hand. It is strong and warm and He smiles as I hold it. He is safe and loving and will not let me down. If we walk together today I will get to know Him better.

Because of my deeper spiritual connections, I was experiencing new levels of meaning in other areas as well. While attending noon Mass at the Albany Cathedral several times a week, I started to get to know a priest who said daily Mass, Simon Mohr, OFM Conv.

I enjoyed the spiritual and practical nature of his homilies very much. On the day that we read the Gospel story of the Road to Emmaus, my friend Marian was also there, and we walked together up the hill to our respective offices after Mass. For several years, Marian and I had been performing an annual puppet show of the Road to Emmaus for children celebrating their First Eucharist at our home parish of Our Lady of Mercy in Colonie, New York. Marian had written the script and I had made the sock puppets, and we enjoyed performing the show as much as the children seemed to enjoy watching it. During his homily that day, Father Simon had encouraged us to pray the prayer the disciples used at Emmaus: "Stay with me Jesus. It's getting dark." Marian and I liked that prayer and wanted to work it into the puppet show. She came up with the wonderful idea to write it on slips of paper, wrap it around small rolls of Lifesaver candies and give them to the children after the show.

And I took that prayer as my own, too, because it seemed to be getting darker in my life. Several facilities had rejected my son and we had rejected several other facilities, for various reasons, so he was still languishing at the shelter. The tutoring there was nominal, the food was fatty, and he was heavily medicated. It was not a good situation. But finally, in April, we seemed to have found a facility that was suitable for him. The only problem was that it was an hour and a half drive away from us. With my health issues and the burden of securing childcare for my younger son if my husband and I were needed for a meeting at the facility, it didn't seem like an ideal situation. But I prayed and spoke with several people I trusted, who said the distance would probably help me to detach from the situation. I was on an antidepressant and Neurontin for pain management, which helped me to stay somewhat level-headed. I am grateful for that, because having to send my son away was tearing me apart inside. I felt like I had failed both him and my family. I was convinced I was a terrible mother and most of his problems had to be my fault. (Now I realize how self-centered that was—to think that I had that much power and control over his behavior.) I found it difficult to let him go, but I did it.

Our younger son was still little and blissfully free of "issues." He and my husband and I went to Holy Saturday services and greatly enjoyed the candlelight, music and rituals. He spoke seriously to me when we went home that Easter eve.

"Mommy, I'm going to be a priest when I grow up."

"You are?" I asked.

"Yes, that's right. And you can wave to me when I'm up there on the altar. But I won't wave back. I'll just smile," he said.

So sweet.

He continued, "And I can bless you all the time if I'm a priest."

"Honey, you will bless me every day of your life just by being the wonderful person that you are," I replied honestly.

During that time, his musical talents also started to become apparent. One day he sat down at a keyboard and played what sounded like a practiced and professional piece of music. I knew he would enjoy formal lessons, and my friend Marian suggested that her daughter Tara, who was one of his babysitters, teach him. They became fast friends, developing a connection that remains in their young adulthood. Through the years he has learned to play several instruments and demonstrated great musical gifts, and has shared his musical talents in several churches.

While attending Mass at Cathedral I had begun to serve on the altar in various capacities when needed. I started as a Eucharistic minister, when Father Pape, the Cathedral Rector, was saying Mass, and they were short one Eucharistic minister. He looked at me and raised his eyebrows and jerked his head as if to say, "Come on, Anne, get over here" so I did: I had no training in being a Eucharistic minister, but I had great reverence and appreciation for the Eucharist. After awhile, I started to hop up as an altar server when Father Simon needed assistance. Some days, I served as a lector. I greatly enjoyed doing all of these things, but I think I enjoyed getting to know Father Simon the most. He started bringing me gifts and I started bringing him baked goods to take home and share with his fellow friars. And so a friendship was born, one that greatly blessed us for many years.

In May of 1998, our prayers for our son began to be answered. I talked to him on the phone often, and at the end of one of our conversations I asked him if he was praying. He said, "Yes, Mom, I pray every day." I reminded him of a conversation we'd had when he was home and very depressed. At that time, he told me that he didn't believe in God, but I promised him that God had a miracle in store for him. That evening, I stated that he had received the miracle I had promised him: he had gotten his faith back. And once again, I realized that God's ways are not my ways.

By Mother's Day I felt blessed. My older son was safe and getting better. His Mother's Day gift to me was a letter he wrote thanking me for all the things I had done for him throughout his life. He said I was a wonderful, caring mother and that he loved me with all his heart. This touched me deeply, especially since he had not acted very loving for several years. I also received beautiful gifts from my younger son and husband. And this year I bought myself a gift as well: an Emerald ring. I had some money saved, so although it seemed extravagant, it did not take anything away from my family. And it was a sign that I was taking care of myself in the midst of difficulties. It was a sign that I was healing. Even now, I smile whenever I put it on.

In the midst of all this, I continued my monthly sessions with Sister Libby, whom I considered a "wisdom woman." She was very practical, down-to-earth and rather acerbic. I still went to her with all my spiritual questions, such as the one I had brought to her the winter before. I was listening to a lot of Christian radio and kept hearing about having a "personal relationship with Jesus." That phrase was not familiar to me, so I broached the topic with her, stating that I didn't know whether I had that or not. After initially responding with "of course, you do, Anne" she seemed thoughtful. A few days later she brought it up in conjunction with another event. There was a severe ice storm, which caused a shortage in ice melt products at local stores. When I found ice melt, I bought an extra bag for Abba House, drove over there in my husband's truck, spread salt on their driveway and stairs, and left the rest of the bag with the sisters. Sister Libby called me on the phone later to tell me that she greatly appreciated what I had done. She also said that it was the type of thing someone who had a personal relationship with Jesus would do. That was the teacher in her: always on the lookout for a way to explain things to me.

Looking back, I see how gentle God has been with me in helping me to heal. I needed a loving and trusting relationship with someone who could be sharp-tongued and brutally honest, and that was Sister Libby. My relationships with strong, outspoken people as a young child had shaped my personality in such a way that I was usually intimidated by strong personalities. But God knew that I needed to be in relationship with a person who had those qualities in order to move forward with my emotional healing.

On a physical level, after years of my own chronic medical issues, I was facing the inevitable solution for my chronic pain: a hysterectomy. I was angry. I took it out on God in my journal, ranting and raving that He could NOT HEAR ME!! I was rather dramatic, listing all of the "work" I had been doing to try to grow spiritually, how well I had been behaving, how strong I'd been with my family situations. Exhausted after a few pages, I wrote:

> My family is torn and broken apart. My health is failing. My faith is floundering. I'm afraid to ask you for help anymore because you don't seem to be answering me at all. This is not a good place to be, Lord. I am not happy. I will go through the motions because they are the right things to do. Maybe I'll find you there somehow.

Part of my anger was because my husband and I had scheduled a trip by ourselves to Florida for a few days, and the trip coincided with an extremely painful menstrual cycle, so I spent most of the time there curled up in the dark hotel room. The migraine headaches I had suffered for years were becoming more frequent, and the loss of the vacation that my husband and I had been looking forward to and desperately needed convinced me to have the hysterectomy. We scheduled it for late July.

****

In June, our son came home for a visit from the residential treatment facility. We saw great improvement in how he handled difficulties, noting that he was able to talk about his frustrations rather than keeping them inside. I was still on edge as I watched for a return of old behaviors, but I did not see them. Instead, I once again saw evidence of my prayers having been answered. At work I looked, in amazement, at the prayer on my desk; I had prayed it dozens of times each day as I fielded calls from his school, doctors, social workers and other professionals: "All shall be well and all will be well and all manner of things shall be well." Whereas in the past I had prayed it desperately, now I prayed it with gratitude, seeing how "well" things were becoming.

During this time I also struggled with the desire to write. I felt called to write but could not seem to complete anything publishable. I frequently wrote in my journal about the desire I had to write, and how I felt that God was leading me to it. But there were so many other things occurring in my life that required my attention. I did write at work, which I later realized helped fulfill my creative needs. And I wrote to God in my prayer journal every day.

Another issue I struggled with most of my life that seemed particularly challenging at this time was overeating. I wrote about that a lot in the pages of my journal through the years, expressing guilt when I overate—always in the evening. Now it seems that I wasted far too much energy on this issue. But I also knew that the overeating was an escape, as well as a learned behavior. I had learned some of my unhealthy eating habits in my family of origin, and habits ingrained from childhood are difficult to break. At this particular point in my life, I was worried about gaining weight before the surgery and then not being able to take it off afterward. This turned out to be another of the many things that I worried about but that never occurred. I actually lost weight during my recuperation period.

As time moved closer to the hysterectomy the pain seemed to increase. I tried very hard to look for the blessings in my situation:

> Dear Lord, please help me to see the blessings in my illness.
> Reveal to me the changes you have willed in my life that have come about because of the pain.
> Help me to see the goodness in people, revealed to me by their empathy.
> Show me the abundance of grace I receive through the many wonderful people in my life.
> Help me to appreciate all that you've given me.

I had been studying the daily Catholic Mass readings for some time. I usually wrote a verse that captured my heart during prayer on a piece of paper and carried it with me through the day. Sometimes I would give the verse to someone I met when it fit into our conversation. I took it out and read it when I was standing in line in a store, sitting in traffic, or while taking a break at my desk. I was learning that I found most of the answers to my problems in the Bible.

In my journal I would write about the daily readings if I felt God was showing me something I did not know or reinforcing something I already knew. When the reading was about Elijah running from God I was charmed. God showed Elijah that He was a God of gentleness: He was not in the fire or the wind, but in a tiny whispering sound. Then after this beautiful enlightenment, God gave Elijah more work to do! I couldn't help but notice that seems to be the way with God: there is always so much more work to do in His kingdom. But that is good: we never have to worry about being bored!

****

At times I was profoundly sad about my impending hysterectomy. I had always wanted a daughter. I cherished my relationship with my mother and grandmother, and so looked forward to having a girl child in my life someday. I grieved this loss for a very long time. For years, I couldn't even look at a baby without crying. But I know that God rewards us double for everything we've lost, so I trust there will be special little girls in my life again someday.

In my darkest moments, I turned to God in prayer and He comforted me. One day I went to Centering Prayer and felt Him holding and rocking me. I cried and He held me and we rocked. When I rose to leave my chair, I took this phrase with me: "Remember how much I love you." During the day I noticed all the loving messages I received from others. At the noon Mass homily, the priest told us to think about how much God loves us. A friend of mine at work encouraged me to go to the nurse's office during the work day and lay down when I did not feel well. She said I put on a brave front. Another friend, who had struggled with forgiving himself, told me that he was finally realizing how much God loves Him. And my husband was particularly gentle and patient with me. God speaks to us in prayer and through people. Even though these were challenging times, I was greatly blessed.

The connections I had with others were deepening. My mother called me often and offered to come and stay with me when I returned from the hospital. I appreciated connecting with her as she, too, had a hysterectomy when she was in her thirties. My friendship with Father Simon was also deepening, and he brought me spiritual books and shared stories of his open heart surgery. He made me laugh, which I needed, and he was affectionate with me in a brotherly way. When I served on the altar with him he would kiss me at the sign of peace. Sometimes he would straighten my collar or pat my cheek. And when we talked he would take my hands and occasionally kiss them. I always felt so cared for when I was with him.

Before the surgery I brought my younger son to Abba House to meet Sister Libby and Sister Mary Gen in September. He was very cute, just a little guy who was open and loving. We prayed together and he shared saltwater taffy with them. I remember him reaching up and popping one into Sister Libby's mouth, and then the quiet afterward when all of our mouths were so full of chewy candy that we could not talk. It was a comfortable quiet. It felt good to have him in the House.

Sister Libby asked me to give a presentation as part of their fall programs: "Stepping Stones in Spiritual Growth." I was excited at the prospect of talking about my faith with other adults. Adult faith sharing grew into a great love for me as the years went on and I became a catechist in an intergenerational faith formation program in my parish. Sister Libby recognized and nourished my ability to be an adult educator: she coaxed it out of me. That's one of the characteristics of a soul friend.

Abba House—Sister Libby's Miracle—In Their Own Words

Written by Sister Libby, published in RSCJ Newsletter, November 1986

This past summer I experienced serious illness and surgery for the first time in my adult life. It was an experience of "amazing grace" from start to finish. During my recuperation, Nance O'Neil [the RSCJ Provincial] came to visit me and asked "Were you able to pray during these past weeks?" I answered yes and no, for no prayer in the usual manner was possible because of the energy it takes to focus on God. I didn't have any. But the "yes" part of the answer came from the experience of utterly simple new ways to pray.

The first serious moment occurred when I had a semi-surgical disagreeable procedure called a lung biopsy. Lying face-down on a table with an X-ray machine flicking back and forth over me while a needle was being placed in my left lung, I experienced acute fear and loneliness. Before I could put that into a prayer, the Lord Himself repeated in my heart: "I am never alone for the Father is always with me."

A day later, the doctor visited me at 9:00 p.m. to tell me they had found some small malignancy and I would need lung surgery. She wanted to prescribe Valium so I could sleep, but I wanted to face it closely and alone with God. So I took my cross (a little plain metal thing which I had with me), lay back on the pillow with it clasped in my hand, said nothing (that I can recall) to God, but fell asleep for six hours—the longest sleep I'd had in my whole hospital experience. It was as the sleep of abandonment to His will and I'm sure He knew it.

A few days later came the rite of reconciliation and the sacrament of the sick prayed with a good priest friend, Father Paul Roman, and Sister Mary Gen Smyth. It was a strengthening experience which filled me with peace.

Terror returned, however, on the day of the surgery while I was being wheeled into an operating room where I had previously assisted as a nurse. I was wide awake in spite of sedation. However, as I was told to extend first one arm and then the other onto waiting boards, I was suddenly filled with a sense of likeness to Jesus on the cross. But again the anesthesiologist began his injection before I even had a word to say to God. The outcome of the surgery was five days in ICU full of hyper activity around me and on me, and utter weakness and pain within me. But each day the chaplains or Eucharistic ministers would bring Communion. As soon as I received, I would fall asleep almost immediately and have my best rest periods, whatever time this occurred. The prayer of sleep!

Next came God's surprise. The malignancy removed from my lung was sent to the pathology lab for evaluation which was to lead to a decision about types of chemotherapy, radiation, etc., to say nothing about a prognosis about my expected life span! However, the malignancy in the sample entirely disappeared. Further tests on me and all kinds of double-checking and anxiety on the part of doctors occurred. Finally all of them said that something inexplicable and mysterious had taken place—so, no chemo, no radiation, no more cancer in me, and a very hopeful future! To experience the Lord's healing touch in such a manner silenced me into a wordless grateful joy that left me and most of the medical world around me speechless. How close can He come? Really!

The surgery left me weakened for a good six weeks—in the hospital for two of them and at home for about four more. I daily received Communion and experienced the Lord as the source of much-needed physical and psychological strength, for surgery wounds our psyche, too, and leaves us fearful about ever feeling "normal" again. Once more, it was a wordless and brief clinging to Him who is the source of ALL that we need, not only the spiritual things we usually pray for. I had never prayed for physical healing for myself, for instance.

It is now three months and I feel fine again, physically and psychologically. I have resumed almost all my usual "works" and my usual prolonged periods of quiet prayer. Reading Scripture again is another great joy. I find verification in these sacred writings for all that has happened to me—in these words which had often "floated through" my weary mind in the previous weeks. Yes, we can pray during sickness, but perhaps it is more accurate to say that *it is He who prays within us* when we are too weak to initiate anything. Blessed be He. Amen.

(Sister Margaret Williams, RSCJ stayed with Sister Libby after her lung surgery, while Sister Mary Gen went on her three month study grant trip to Israel, Egypt and Greece in 1986.)

ABBA HOUSE—GATHERINGS AND PROGRAMS

During the 1970's

When the Abba Community was in its early years, in the 1970's, the Sisters focused most of their energy on offering a place where people could be prayerful rather than on formal programs. In fact, a document found in the archives "Abba Community Begins Second Year" dated 1972 describes the House of Prayer as a place of quiet that did not offer formal programs.

> It seems that most Christians today, whether lay or religious, need to step aside from full activity from time to time and go to a place of quiet to re-achieve integration and refreshment. The core members try to provide this spirit by their own prolonged prayer and simple lifestyle. For this reason too, they have chosen to avoid formal programs and multiple activities and offerings, believing that prayer itself is a form of service in the church. At the same time the House of Prayer is an open and welcoming place quite different from the cloisters of former days. In it Christians from all walks of life can enrich one another and grow more deeply in the love of God and man.

From this root of individual and community prayer, it was a natural growth to the House serving as a gathering place for groups from different communities whose focus was prayer and the spiritual life. Within a few years after its establishment at Kenwood in 1971, groups began using the Abba House of Prayer as a meeting place for prayer and gatherings. Some of those groups were the Graymoor Friars, the LaSalette seminarians, Marriage Encounter Groups, Catholic Singles and the faculty of a number of Catholic schools. Overnight stays were encouraged as well, first at Kenwood and then at Western Avenue. Both facilities had several guest rooms that were offered to Religious of different communities and lay people. Guests came for days of prayer, annual retreats or sabbaticals composed of quiet study and prayer. When the small community moved to Western Avenue in 1973, they welcomed neighbors who dropped in to pray or attend the liturgies offered at the House three to four times each week.

Another important role of Abba House was to be a support to the Roman Catholic parishes of the Albany Diocese. The Sisters opened their doors to many parish groups for retreats and gatherings, Confirmation candidates, youth groups, Rite of Christian Initiation of Adults (RCIA) groups, RENEW Groups, and staff. Those parishes included Our Lady of Mercy, St. Vincent de Paul, St. Andrew's Episcopal, St. Margaret Mary, Holy Cross, St. Catherine of Siena, St. Madeleine Sophie, St. Adalbert, St. Edward, St. Monica, St. John the Baptist, and many others. In addition, the Sisters traveled to many of the same parishes and others to present talks on prayer, spirituality and Bible Studies.

A January 1975 letter from the Abba Community to the Religious of the Sacred Heart described some of the Community's activities outside of the House that brought them into neighboring faith communities. Those activities included speaking to Rosary societies at several parishes, giving Days of Recollection at the Episcopalian cathedral and visiting the sick as Eucharistic ministers in the nearby parish where they were congregants. Bible studies were a large part of their early ministry. From 1975 to 1992, they consistently offered Bible classes each week, at both Abba House and at St. Paul's in Schenectady. For several years, they offered a Bible study series at up to five different locations.

In the mid-1970's, the Abba Community began providing a New Year's Eve celebration with a spiritual bent at the House, an offering that continued annually for several decades. Sr. Libby would create a program for the evening consisting of Scripture readings, prayer responses, silence and music. The program was always connected to current events on both a local and global level. People would start arriving at 9 pm, and the program would start at 10 pm, after which guests were encouraged to disperse throughout the House for some individual quiet prayer and reflection. Everyone returned to the basement for liturgy at midnight. Following Mass, light snacks were offered upstairs, followed by time for fellowship until about 2 am. Mary Ellen Colfer, a friend of the House who both attended and led programs at Abba House, remembers one of those celebrations in particular.

> One New Year's Eve I joined the gathering of folks who had come to share stories and song and to 'pray in the New Year centered in Jesus Christ.' I brought a song to share that night which offered a way of praying with gentle movement in a circle and extending peace to all the nations of the world. It was a profound experience as the group moved together and sang as the name of every nation of the world was called out. There was one man from a foreign country present that night, and he was deeply touched as he realized his nation was being prayed for so far away from his home. The Holy Spirit truly blessed in surprising and special ways each one who came to Abba House!

One of the groups that met regularly at Abba House for several years in the mid 1970's was the Diocesan Search program. The program offered teenagers from the Albany Diocese a structured program to help them search and find Jesus and develop their own personal relationship with Him. For a weekend at a time, Abba House took in groups of up to 35 young people under the supervision of Diocesan staff. The young men would sleep in the finished basement and the girls slept on the upper two floors. Abba House hosted the program for three years and several hundred young people from the Diocese attended. According to Sister Mary Gen, one of the factors in the Abba Community's move from the Kenwood grounds to their own house on Western Avenue was the influence of Father John J. Rooney, who coordinated the Search Program. He was a supporter of the Community and envisioned them in a home-like setting where the young people in the Search Program could stay for retreats. Since Abba House had a home-like feel to it, he thought the young people might be more apt to take what they learned at the House through the Search program back into their own homes. That desire led him to help the Sisters find an appropriate house for their community: 647 Western Avenue.

In April of 1975, at the two-year point of the relationship between the Search Program and Abba House, James Reinhardt, Assistant Youth Director at the Roman Catholic Diocese, wrote a letter to Sister Libby that summed up their relationship. The letter expressed gratitude to Sister Libby and the Abba Community for their visible service of room and board, as well as the deeper ministry they provided to the young people participating in the Search Program.

> It has something to do with support, with caring, with prayer, with providing a setting where young people can feel the presence of the Spirit in their lives. It also has to do with the witness that you and the other sisters give. The Search program seems to be such an important event in the lives of the young people who take part in it—new discoveries and awareness-es, about themselves, about other people, about God in their lives, about their relationship to the Church—and it is happening in a prayerful, supporting setting [or, perhaps it is happening because of a prayerful, supporting setting!]...I can't imagine this happening like it does anywhere but at Abba House.

Search Program, Abba House ground floor, circa 1973

During the 1980's

Throughout the 1980's, the ministry of Abba House expanded through private and directed retreats. At any given time, several persons on spiritual sabbaticals of varying lengths could be found living in the community.

One of the first of many local newspaper articles, written on the House's 10th anniversary, was a piece in the July 11, 1981 Schenectady Gazette titled "Abba House Aims to Foster Prayer." The focus of the article was Abba House's primary purpose: to encourage and develop people's prayer lives and strengthen their relationship with God. The following quotes from Sister Libby were included in the article.

- Some people think you have to have a structured method of approaching God when what you need is a trustful openness.
- Some people don't believe God loves them just as they are so they believe they have to win his love by right actions.

- Ten years ago it was the pious types—in the best sense of that word—that came here. There are more people coming now that have been away from the Lord for a long time and need help.
- People are getting more desperate because of all the problems in life. Increasingly people are finding no middle ground anymore between God and despair.

The article also pointed out that, although the major purpose of the House at the beginning of its ministry was to offer spiritual respite to members of religious communities involved in active ministry, it had expanded to include laypersons. In fact, by 1981, lay people comprised eighty to eighty-five percent of all visitors to the House, including an increasing number of those belonging to faith traditions other than Roman Catholic. In the second and third decades of Abba House's thirty year long ministry under Sister Libby and Sister Mary Gen, there was greater emphasis on formal programs like Bible Studies, spiritual enrichment opportunities, spiritual direction and retreats.

In 1985, the Sisters began distributing a formal calendar of upcoming events along with their Letter to Friends. An excerpt from an early letter follows.

> Somehow fall is another New Year's season because so many programs begin everywhere. So we greet you lovingly and give you a description—and a calendar—of what Abba House is offering in 1985-86.
>
> Folded in convenient form, the calendar can be left on your desk or bureau and be a reminder. Those of you who live far away are invited to keep it in a handy place also so that you may pray for spiritual growth for both participants and presenters.

Before they started producing formal calendars, information on program offerings at Abba House was disseminated in a variety of ways, including public service announcements that led to notices in church bulletins and radio announcements, notices in local newspapers, and flyers posted in churches. Program information was also publicized within articles that were written about the Sisters, the House and spiritual matters by several local newspapers. The Sisters mailed their "Letters to Friends" several times each year to keep regular guests updated on offerings: by the time the Sisters left the House in 2001, their mailing list had grown to 1500.

The fall 1985 Letter to Friends quoted above also described new ecumenical involvements with Methodists and Presbyterians and a continuation of their "historic relationship with our Episcopalian brethren." But their ecumenical work was evident from the beginning of their ministry. Just as Abba House served as a meeting place and provided programs to support local Roman Catholic parishes, it supported other denominations as well, especially Episcopal. The Sisters hosted meetings of the Episcopalian seminarians, deacons, wives of ministers and women ministers. Groups from other faith communities that met at Abba House through the years included Methodist and Lutheran ministers, members of the First Congregational and West End Presbyterian congregations, the Council of Churches, the Albany Uptown Churches, ecumenical commissions from several denominations, and many others.

> *"This fall marks a milestone in the life of Abba House of Prayer—a tenth anniversary. We ourselves have trouble believing that we have completed a decade, but no trouble believing that it is entirely due to the providing love of God and the utter goodness and strong faith of so many of you, our generous supporters." September 1981 Letter to Friends*

The fall 1985 letter referenced a workshop the Sisters attended in Syracuse by Father Anthony DeMello, SJ, "the Indian Jesuit" who "gives superb help in becoming AWARE—aware of the presence of God in ourselves and our lives." Sister Mary Gen attended three retreats led by Father DeMello, and she described the experiences as remarkable. She and Sister Libby modeled a number of their presentations after DeMello's spirituality and offered many books, tapes and videos from him in their House, even during the time when his teachings were not supported by the Catholic Church.

Throughout the 30 Year Ministry

Roman Catholic liturgy was an essential part of the House from its start at Kenwood to the time when the sisters left Abba House after 30 years of ministry in 2001-02. When they first started the House at Kenwood they were able to bring priests in to say Mass three or four times per week, but that decreased gradually through the years to a few times per month by the end of their ministry. This decrease correlates with the decrease in the number and availability of priests in the Albany Diocese.

Dozens of priests, including Bishop Howard Hubbard, have fond memories of their times at Abba House where they had dinner with the sisters and any guests staying there and offered Mass in their cozy living room. One of the priests "on rotation" for those early Masses at Abba House was Bishop Hubbard when he was still a priest in the South End of Albany. Through the years, he maintained a steady, supportive relationship with the Abba Community, visiting at least once annually for supper and liturgy. He recalls that his times with the Sisters were always "relaxing, refreshing and renewing."

Liturgy at Abba House, circa 1975, (left to right) Sister Mary Gen, Sister Libby, unidentified guest, Reverend John J. Rooney

A consistent offering at the House for many years was Sister Mary Gen's Spirituality of Daily Life Series, which began with her training to be an At-Home Retreat leader in the late 1970's. An article in the Schenectady Gazette in September of 1981 described the At-Home Retreat movement as following a manual based on the spiritual exercises of St. Ignatius of Loyola, with added flexibility allowed for personal sharing by team leaders. The article named Sister Mary Gen and Mrs. Jean Ryan of Troy as two local At-Home Retreat leaders. The local branch of this effort, focusing on women only, was part of a worldwide movement organized by the Sisters of the Cenacle on Long Island. The program was thirteen weeks long. Groups consisting of six to twelve women met weekly for prayer, sharing spiritual experiences and talks by team leaders. Participants were given scriptures to reflect upon during the week and asked to pray for fifteen minutes each day. This format taught women to integrate prayer into their daily lives and make it habitual. One month after the retreat ended there was a renewal meeting to give the participants a chance to discuss their successes and failures in prayer life and spirituality. This program was popular and successful because it allowed women to develop spiritually in their everyday environments. Due to the length of the program, team leaders interviewed prospective participants prior to joining to help them determine whether they were willing to commit to the entire thirteen weeks.

Out of her experiences with the At-Home Retreat Program, Sister Mary Gen developed a similar eight-week program of instruction and discussion of prayer and spirituality that was offered at Abba House. Called the Spirituality of Daily Life, this was a very popular program for almost 20 years. Sister Mary Gen continued offering the Daily Life Retreat until 2001, and over 100 people completed the series. For a number of years, she also offered a series called Daily Life Retreat II, a six-week course in spirituality for those who had completed the first series and wanted to continue to grow their spirituality in a similar format.

The Memory Book we compiled when the Sisters left the House in 2001 contained a number of entries from people who had attended the Daily Life Retreat over the years. They all wrote how the program had been a life changing experience for them, helping them to develop a practice of daily prayer that had enriched their lives in many different ways.

The following quote from the foundress of the Society of the Sacred Heart, Saint Madeleine Sophie Barat, exemplifies the Abba House Sisters' ever-changing, creative attitude toward personal prayer.

> Only put your soul in contact with Jesus Christ and there is nothing that you cannot become and do. We should pray in any way that we find easiest, easiest and most reasonable, which means based on faith and on a realization of our nothingness before God. The way we want to pray, the way we like to pray, is the way we should pray. So pray in any way that puts you into contact with God.
>
> The Society of the Sacred Heart: History of a Spirit,
> Margaret Williams, RSCJ, p. 327

> *"Sister Libby and Sister Mary Gen were the kinds of religious that really helped build up the church. They had entered the order when it was cloistered and had adjusted well when that ended: they had a witness to the world."*
>
> *Deacon Nancy Rosenblum*

Sister Libby and Sister Mary Gen during the last year of their ministry at Abba House, 2001

My House—Surgery and Recuperation

The surgery that resolved my chronic endometriosis blessed me with the ability to recognize and receive love from many people. The dread and fear I had felt in anticipation of the hysterectomy left no room for the gifts, but God found a way to sneak them in. This was the most difficult surgery I have had, and I have a solid basis of comparison, having undergone five abdominal surgeries. The pain was intense during the recuperation period, and there were complications during the surgery, which further extended that recuperation period. But before I went on leave from work, my co-workers gave a breakfast in my honor, and many friends stopped by to wish me well. There were lots of hugs and kisses and good wishes. After the surgery, I had the gift of my mother visiting me at the hospital, and then staying with me at home for a few days—that was lovely. And there were cards and gifts and flowers and phone calls from many people. If I had ever doubted that I was greatly loved, I did not doubt it any longer.

During my recuperation, I connected with people I did not normally talk to, largely because I was now home during the day. And I had the chance to be the recipient of others' gifts to me—like home visits and rides to places, as I was not able to drive. I learned that when I allowed myself to receive something from someone who cared about me and wanted to give to me, even if it made me uncomfortable, I received a double gift: the shared giving and receiving became a beautiful memory and a bond between us forever.

I had a lot of free time, and began pondering, once again, the possibility of changing careers. I prayed and journaled, asking God to lead me in the direction He wanted me to go. I prayed daily to stay in the center of God's will for my life. As I prayed, I thought about the religious education classes I had been teaching for the past few years. In each class there had been one student with some kind of special needs—one student who was extremely difficult to reach and teach. I was often frustrated during my efforts to teach those particular students, but I knew there must be effective methods to work with them. Exploring my career options in a conversation with a friend one day, she suggested that I consider teaching Special Education. That idea appealed to me, so I began researching jobs in the teaching field. The fact that the retirement systems for government employees and public school teachers allowed for transfer of time between the two systems helped my husband support my interest. We researched pay scales for beginning public school teachers and, while the rates were significantly lower than my current position, I rationalized that the transition would be less painful because it would be from part-time in my then current job to full-time as a teacher. Our family could survive financially, although teaching was not nearly as lucrative as the career track I was on. As the financial provider for our home, my husband struggled with my decision, but eventually conceded to the plan because he wanted me to be happy and was fully aware of my dissatisfaction with my job situation at the time.

There were several reasons for my wanting to become a teacher: I wanted to use my talents in God's service in a field where I could make a difference; I felt "called" to teach children who could be difficult to teach; and I wanted to escape my work situation. I also had empathy for the parents of my future students, as I was the parent of a young person with special needs who had been struggling in the education system.

As I began to seriously consider changing careers, Sister Libby suggested that I take small steps, and if it were God's will that I continue on this path, the way would be made clear. So I began by making an appointment with the Admissions office at The College of Saint Rose. I learned that I would have to get a Master's Degree in order to be marketable. I was pleased to find out that if I started soon and studied for three years I could graduate with a Master's Degree in Education in 2001. I would also receive my degree before a new requirement by the New York State Education Department that called for Master's Degree candidates in education to become certified in the same fields as their undergraduate degree (my undergraduate degree was in English and Journalism, not Special Education). When I learned about the fortuitous timing, I took it as a sign from God that I was on the right path.

****

In the fall my husband was asked to lead a RENEW Group at our church, as a leader of a small faith-sharing group. The pastoral minister at our church, Sister Yvette, said she got the idea to ask him when she visited me in the hospital after my hysterectomy and saw him there. To my surprise, he accepted her invitation. Since I had been reading the Bible daily for several years, I offered to help him, but he refused, saying that if he wanted my help he would ask for it. I was hurt and resentful. In my journal I wrote that I had waited so long to share the Word of God with him and now that the opportunity seemed to have arrived, his pride was in the way. But was my reaction my own pride? I was focusing on how my own needs were not being met in our relationship rather than being grateful that my husband was taking advantage of an opportunity to grow in his faith and to make new connections at church.

Realizing that I was making myself miserable, I decided to take care of myself, both spiritually and physically. I realized that I was choosing not to become involved in the RENEW groups because I continued to be deeply involved in catechesis. I decided to teach a fifth grade religious education class, which was a different age level than I had taught in the past, and I greatly enjoyed it. I also started receiving Healing Touch sessions at my doctor's suggestion because I had not fully recuperated from my hysterectomy. Those sessions both helped me to heal and introduced me to a gift I did not know I had: several years later, fascinated with Healing Touch, I began taking classes and learned that I am a healer. Once again, something beautiful was born out of pain and difficult times.

In spite of my best efforts at wellness, I was feeling stressed. I was having a difficult time regulating my hormone replacement dosage, which I needed after experiencing a complete hysterectomy while still in my thirties: too low of a dose resulted in hot flashes and aching joints, too high and I was jittery and anxious. I still had residual abdominal pain from the surgery and occasional bladder infections because my bladder was not fully emptying due to surgical complications. I was overeating as a response to the stress I felt from the slow healing and the challenges our family was having with our older son when he came to visit every few weeks. My husband and I were seeing some regression in his behaviors that concerned us. In the late fall, I decided I needed to get myself back to Abba House for some spiritual and physical rest and peace.

While I was there, I realized that I had been somewhat depressed for several months. During my spiritual direction, Sister Libby spoke about the difference gratitude can make in our lives. In her down-to-earth fashion she commented that our society seemed to need a support group for everything, mentioning that she had heard about a group for "empty nesters" who were having a hard time with their children leaving for college. She said, "why don't they read a book or something and get over it—be grateful that their children are going to college?" (There was that sharp sensibility/impatience of hers.) I took the gratitude comment to my room with me and decided to make a gratitude list. This is what it looked like.

I am grateful for:

my husband and my children
relatively good health
my parents
my brother and his family
my job
teaching religious education
plenty to eat and wear
my house

music
sunshine
Abba House
my van
Mass
books
my fellowship with others
different priorities than what I used to have
my grandmother
my step-grandchildren
my son's safety
clean air
the love of my husband
being able to write
to pray
to teach
to draw
to sew
to hug and kiss
to sing
to kneel and thank You
I am grateful for
my husband's encouragement,
his wonderful attitude,
his strength and good health
my older son's growth and acceptance
my younger son's loving and happy nature
my nieces' unconditional love
my mother's support
my father's laughter
all the abundance in my life
all the joy in my life
all the pain in my life because it is making me stronger.
I am grateful for
finding you again after losing you for so long.
I am grateful for
your open arms and gentle touch,
the friends and messages you send me

and the insights you lead me to.
I am grateful for
showing me how much you love me
and how valuable I am to you and others.
I am grateful for
allowing myself to feel my feelings
the courage to reach out to others
the freedom to do as I want
the options I have
the choices I make
the love I know.
I am grateful for
safety
lack of oppression
the neighborhood I live in
the changing seasons
the children in my life.
I am grateful that
I can be trusted
people love me
people like me
I'm not alone.
So this is where you've been, Lord—
Trapped inside my selfishness.
Gratitude sets you free.
I notice that the sun is shining.
Things are better now.

While at Abba House for those few days, I also started working on the presentation on group prayer experiences that I had agreed to do as part of their Stepping Stones in Spiritual Growth series. Preparing and presenting on this topic was a rich experience for me. First I prayed about it, then I pondered my different prayer experiences. In spending quiet time putting them together, I was able to reflect deeply on the times I had prayed with others. Writing about spiritual experiences—like writing this book—is incredibly rewarding. It's almost like re-living the blessed times but standing off a bit and watching them unfold retrospectively as a third party.

The group prayer times I wrote about didn't seem significant individually, but putting them all together made them very special. One is praying with fellow catechists: it seems to have a vibration to it, like meditating in a group or practicing yoga with people you have known for awhile. Sharing and teaching about God's love brings a distinctive energy to the room. Praying with children is very moving; their innocence and vulnerability is sweet and their faces seem to shine with the light of God's love. Praying with my family has always been profound to me: there is already much love there and when we invite reciprocal divine energy it is so beautiful it can make me cry. Writing about these experiences and others and then talking about them with a group made me extremely appreciative. I would not have had these insights had it not been for Sister Libby, who both invited me to make the presentation and took part in it.

****

During the next few weeks I felt confused, as if I were at a crossroads. We were preparing for my older son's permanent return home from residential treatment and were apprehensive. Still healing from my hysterectomy, I tired easily and felt overwhelmed by the advice I was getting from different people, both about my son's return and my exploration of a new career. Following Sister Libby's suggestion, I decided to submit an application to graduate school and watch the process to see how it flowed. If it moved relatively easily, I would take that as a sign that it was meant to be.

At Thanksgiving I felt blessed and grateful. The previous year I had missed the family Thanksgiving dinner because I was at the hospital with my son. This year he was with us and much healthier than he had been in years. I think this was the first time I celebrated Thanksgiving with a true spirit of gratitude, not taking anyone's inventory or expecting family members to meet any of my pre-meditated expectations.

Christmas came shortly after celebrating my son's 15th birthday (along with Sister Libby's birthday). It was a peaceful Christmas, with family differences set aside in order to focus on the reason for the season. We went to Mass together on Christmas

Eve, and had a joyful Christmas morning with gifts and lots of love. When I returned to work on the 29th I wrote: "Back to work today. I will work in prayer and make my work a prayer and do the very best I can. It will be my gift to you today, Lord."

ABBA HOUSE—DAYS OF PRAYER

The Lord God has given me a well-trained tongue, that I might know how to speak to the weary a word that will rouse them. Isaiah 50:4

During the 1980's and into the 1990's, Days of Prayer were popular offerings at Abba House. The typical format for a Day of Prayer was a "talk" on a given topic, usually provided by a guest speaker. Attendees brought their own bag lunch, and were given time for private reflection. The day often ended in Catholic Liturgy. An example of a Day of Prayer offered in October 1986 was titled "Relaxing with the Lord." It opened with a welcome and prayer led by Sister Libby, followed Father Jim Kane's talk, "Relaxing with the Scriptures." Then there was "quiet time" followed by liturgy. After a brown bag lunch, there was another presentation, this one given by author Margaret Williams, RSCJ, called "Let us go off by ourselves to a lonely place where we can be alone and rest for awhile." It was based on a Scriptural reference to Jesus' call to his apostles following a busy period of ministry.

Lenten and Advent Days of Prayer were annual offerings for many years. Topics for Advent Days of Prayer included "Discovering a 20th Century Mary," "Praying the Advent Scriptures," and "Sharing Ideas for Observing Advent and Avoiding the Secular Christmas Fever." Other Days of Prayer included one on the spirituality of joy (also led by Sister Margaret Williams) and one given by a married clergy couple on the topic of prayer as the chief bond in a marriage and in all loving and communal relationships.

During 1987-88, the Program included some Days of Prayer tailored to specific groups, including a day dedicated to senior citizens, one for single adults and one for office workers. For several years, the sisters offered programs for nurses, such as "Discovering Our Personal Giftedness and Sharing It," which included a closing prayer service aptly titled "healing love." The Abba House 1987 annual Letter to Friends mentioned they were asked by three social workers to host a monthly evening of meditation and sharing for victims of AIDS. In 1988-89, they offered a series of five "Couples Nights" programs throughout the year. These were follow-up meetings to the Marriage Encounter group that Sister Libby and Mary Gen attended together.

Seasonal offerings were common, such as a May 1986 spring Day of Prayer, called "Reflections on Nature." The day included two talks by Sister Mary Gen, an object meditation by Sister Libby, Liturgy with Walter Laskos, OFM, lunch, two quiet times, and "Audio-Visual Spirituality" (video presentation) on the "Beauty of Nature in Prayer." This quote by Ralph Waldo Emerson was used in the program flyer:

> Never lose an opportunity for seeing anything that is beautiful;
> For beauty is God's handwriting—a wayside sacrament.
> Welcome it in every fair face, in every fair sky, in every fair flower,
> And thank God for it as a cup of His blessing.

Father Paul Roman led many programs at Abba House through the years. He moved to different parishes in the Capital District, but, as he put it, "wherever I was, they found me!" He also invited the Sisters to come and visit him in his various locations. He shared a memory with me about a prayer experience he asked the Sisters to lead when he was living in Oneonta. As in the program above, those attending were asked go outside and find a rock to bring back and use during an object meditation. Father Roman said that the men were angry because they had expected "nuns in habits" and "traditional stuff" and some of them complained that they didn't want to "go off and find a rock." In Father Roman's words, "I lost my cool. I pulled a crucifix out around my neck and showed them a rock right next to the crucifix and said 'See this? God is the ROCK of my salvation!'" He loved the Sisters.

Some of the program offerings focused on specific topics. In 1988, an Evening of Prayer was held in honor of Saint Rose Philippine Duchesne, RSCJ, who was canonized July 3, 1988. She was one of the founding members of the Society of the Sacred Heart, the order to which that both Sister Libby and Sister Mary Gen belonged, as well as the missionary who brought the Society to America. She was also known as "The Woman Who Prays Always." That evening included a presentation by Lucie Nordmann, RSCJ and Liturgy offered by Rev. James Kane using the official text for the Liturgy of the new saint. An example of a topical series was "Music as a Ladder to Prayer" which featured four different musical topics with four different gifted local musicians leading each evening's presentation. Another topic for a series was "Jesus and Women," which consisted of a series of tapes by Rosemary Haughton and other women authors.

> *"Clearly we are a small facility more remarkable for a personal approach and for promoting fellowship and community in our groups rather than for gathering crowds. But we are inspired by a quotation from St. Rose Philippine Duchesne, the first woman of our religious congregation to come to the USA from France in 1817. 'We cultivate a very small field for Christ, but we love it, knowing that God does not require great achievements but a heart that holds back nothing.'" September 1991 Letter to Friends*

The Sisters' growing ecumenical charism became more visible in their program offerings as the years passed. In the 1980's, they offered several days of prayer for "Episcopalians and Others" led by Abba House Board member Reverend Delos Wampler. They also offered an evening of prayer for "Episcopalians and Others" with Deacon Nancy Rosenblum. Another ecumenical offering led by Deacon Rosenblum was an afternoon of prayer and reflection titled "A Chariot to God," based on the writings of Rabbi Nachman, a 19th century Jewish mystic. In the late 1980's, Abba House began offering yearly interfaith days of prayer where persons of different faith traditions, including Muslim, Hindu and Buddhist, were invited to spend an afternoon of prayer, sharing of common concerns, and sociability.

> *"Abba House was a very peaceful place. Sister Libby and Sister Mary Gen were women of prayer and very practical. They showed people that you didn't have to go into a convent to be a person of prayer."*
>
> *Deacon Nancy Rosenblum*

Series/Regular Programs

In addition to the regular Bible studies, some of the program offerings during the year were also Scripture-based, such as a six week series during Lent of 1999 titled "How the Bible Teaches us to Handle Stress," and a four week series that same year called "Women in the Bible." I was a presenter at the latter series, on "Women in the Early Church." I focused on four women from the New Testament: Lydia, Priscilla, Dorcas (aka Tabitha) and Phoebe, with particular emphasis on Lydia. In an excerpt from my talk I discussed Lydia's dedication to her faith.

> All of us here tonight bring our life experience to our work in the faith. As catechists, parents, friends, ministers in various capacities in the church, all of us are a sum of many parts. Our work in the business world is valuable because we learn important lessons there, just as Lydia did. And God rejoices in the integration of our experiences—our ability to draw from this or that experience to further his work on earth.
>
> Lydia's time by the river demonstrated her desire to strike a balance between work and prayer. Just as we come here to Abba House and go to our churches, prayer groups and

> other faith communities, Lydia took time from her busy life as a businesswoman to feed her spirit with the Word of God in the company of other believers.
>
> This businesswoman, this seller of purple, this Gentile woman with an open heart and a loving spirit, was the first baptized Christian in Europe. Later in Acts, we read that after Paul and Silas are arrested, beaten and imprisoned, then miraculously freed by an angel of the Lord, they returned to Lydia's house, where they were once again welcomed. So Lydia's house church remained a haven of hospitality and an important hub of the early church in Philippi. Lydia's dedication resulted in an abundant harvest for the Kingdom of God.

I see many similarities between Lydia's "house church" and Abba House: both were led by prayerful, loving women and filled with hospitality, prayer and hope. And after doing the research for this book it is very clear that Abba House resulted in an abundant harvest for the Kingdom of God!

In the late 1980's, the Abba House programs began to include more series formats, which built community by bringing the same interested core of attendees together repeatedly for different program components. In 1988-89, the Sisters introduced two new series, one in the fall on "Spiritual Writers" (Thomas Merton, Karl Rahner, Anthony DeMello, Henri Nouwen) and one in the spring entitled "Exploring Lay Spirituality." Both were offered several times throughout the 1990's. Their series format continued into the early 1990's with a program on American Culture/Christian Values, a four week reflection group led by Sr. Libby and based on the book Habits of the Heart by Robert N. Bellah. Another, "Simplicity of Life" led by Walt Chura, was offered several times throughout the 1990's, and studied the lives of St. Francis of Assisi, St. Therese of Lisieux, the Shaker Movement and the Catholic Worker Movement.

In the fall of 1988, Abba House began hosting a monthly meeting at the request of some people in Twelve Step programs who wanted a closer relationship with their "Higher Power" or

God as they understood Him/Her. The group was made up of recovering people, some of whom were comfortable in organized religion and others who were not affiliated with organized religion for various reasons. Abba House was a place where people in recovery could blend their reliance on Twelve Step tenets with a Christian view of a "Higher Power." The meeting was an informal faith-sharing group that gathered for about ninety minutes, with leadership rotating between the Abba House sisters and the participants. Between six and twenty people usually attended, and the program was offered regularly until 2001.

Peace and justice were prevalent themes in many of the programs offered at the House. One of the series the Sisters developed was simply called "Praying Together," and it met three times throughout each year over the course of three years: Praying Together Part One promoted peace among nations, Part Two promoted non-violence in ourselves and our society and Part Three dealt with overcoming addictive behaviors. They offered a series on peace and justice in the early 1990's developed by Barbara DiTommaso entitled "Jesus Set His Face Toward Jerusalem." The sisters also developed a four week series on controlling violence "within ourselves and around us" taken from a Scripture based program "Putting Down Stones" that originated with the Sojourners Community.

Many of the programs offered spiritual assistance for ordinary daily life, such as "Ideas of God and their Effect on our Prayer," "the Bible and Life Cycles" and "How the Bible Teaches us to Handle Stress." The sisters put a spiritual spin on the millennium by offering "Christian Agenda for AD 2001" which included ideas and projections about the future church based on taped lectures by Richard McBrien, Eugene LaVerdiere and Bernard Haring (the Redemptorist priest who inspired the House of Prayer movement in the late 1960's). Sometimes the sisters formed retreat groups that met on a regular basis for a period of several weeks. One example was a six week group retreat called "Pentecost Teachings" which met weekly; another was a study and discussion group called "Connecting Faith and Life."

Similar to the series-type programs, the sisters used "themes" to build community among their guests. It wasn't unusual for them to weave three or four themes together during a single year, with each including a series of three to four programs. Over all of these would be a larger umbrella topic, such as Prayer or Ministry. The topic during 1994-95 was "Seeking Prayer, Quiet and Peace in a Busy World." Toward the end of their thirty-year ministry, they enlisted the aid of Board members on a Program Committee to help with the program formation.

> *"We are also involving people from all walks of life as presenters because that is the real church of today and tomorrow. Please pray that God's grace flows through all of us to all of you." September 1988 Letter to Friends*

The Sisters were very much aware of the changes in the "people's church" as the number of priests and religious gradually decreased over the years. In support of the necessity for lay people to take a more active role in church leadership, they enlisted more and more lay leaders for their program offerings. Several of their Letters to Friends during the 1990's referenced a model of collaborative ministry described in Bishop Hubbard's book on that topic, Fulfilling the Vision. I was fortunate enough to offer three separate programs at Abba House, one of which was a component in the series "Stepping Stones to Spiritual Growth." This was a four week series consisting of Scripture Study, Group Prayer Experiences (me), Spiritual Guidance and Ways to Make a Retreat.

Here is a synopsis of the sisters' final program during their last year together (September 2000 to April 2001—their thirtieth year).

Overall theme: Touching God in Daily Life
I. God in Daily Life and People
II. God in Imagination and Symbols (Words, Images Videos)
III. God in Art and Music (Various Forms)
IV. God in Human Activity (Ministry and Service to Others).

I presented one of the evening components of the "God in Daily Life and People" series, and the focus for my presentation was "People Raising Families." That evening is a sweet memory for me, since my husband attended. I also remember my theme for the evening, "God is in the house!!" which I repeated enthusiastically and often during the presentation.

My House—Mama Goes Back to School

I was accepted into graduate school at The College of Saint Rose and started my coursework in January 1999. My first class, an introduction to individuals with disabilities, was taught by a wonderful woman who worked for a local BOCES (Board of Cooperative Education Services). I was the oldest person in the class and the only parent of a person with disabilities. The instructor was delighted to have me present because I brought a perspective that would benefit teachers in training: I was a parent much like the ones they would be dealing with throughout their careers. In that class, I learned that I would be bringing something of great value to my teaching: the empathy and understanding of a parent whose greatest concern was the well-being of the student.

On a spiritual level, this was a great awakening. I started to understand that our greatest gifts and gains in life often result from our greatest brokenness. The anxiety I continued to experience over my son's inability to handle situations that other people's children seemed to sail through was very painful. The fear I had about his future and ability to function independently in the world was real. The stress and sadness our family dealt with on a nearly daily basis was a hard reality. But these difficult emotions gifted me with a great compassion for others going through similar situations. And, as my son and our family moved through repeated crises by asking for and receiving help from professionals, friends and relatives, I also began to grow in faith that all would be well, eventually. It would be difficult, but it would be okay. And that message of hope was a beautiful thing to bring to both the parents of young people with disabilities and to the students themselves.

In addition to a new start for my professional life through attendance at graduate school, the new year brought a new promise: our son was coming home. I had some concerns, but also recognized that the entire family had grown emotionally and spiritually during the year he was away. He had learned new coping mechanisms, and my husband and I had taken some time to explore the strengths and weaknesses of our own relationship. As a family we had learned better communication skills, which slowed our reaction times and enabled us to act rather than react more often when stressors arose.

It felt like a precarious time, when the slightest misstep could throw us off balance, and I was praying my heart out. My journal showed the pervasiveness of my prayer and how I was learning to invite God into every aspect of my life. I am convinced it was prayer that kept us together as a family. We have prayed together, increasingly more as the years have passed. I prayed/wrote this after a difficult weekend when our son had visited:

> Oh God, please give my husband and me the strength and the wisdom to deal with these situations the way you would. Show us the most effective ways. I know that your way can be difficult, so I am prepared for that. It's the end result I am concerned about. And give us the fortitude to walk your path without becoming angry with each other. I love you and trust you now. You've shown me that your way is best. Please continue to walk with our family.

A week later, the family was edgy and apprehensive as another weekend visit from our son approached, with his permanent return date only a week away. My prayers increased:

> Dear Lord,
>
> Please help us to remember that we are a family. You made us a family to love and support each other, not drive each other away. Please give us patience and keep

> us calm; help us to not take things personally. We're not always aware of how much we hurt each other.
>
> We will be needing your gift of forgiveness more and more, because we will make mistakes. Show us how to forgive so that we do not hold grudges against one another.
>
> Help us to speak softly to one another, not to speak with anger or bitterness. Maybe if we do we'll remember how much we really love each other.
>
> And finally, give us your greatest gift: faith. We need to believe that everything will be alright as long as we do our parts. It will not be perfect, but it will be well.
>
> Thank you for hearing my prayer.

It was about this time that I started ending most of my journal entries with "thank you for hearing my prayer." It showed the beginning of an increased faith and acceptance of God's will.

****

As my husband's and my tenth wedding anniversary approached in April, I began to see a change in the way I measured our years together. My husband is thirty years older than I, and up to that point, I had been very fearful of losing him. I remember, about five years into my marriage, telling a good friend that I wasn't sure how I would handle his death. She was a woman of great faith, a single parent raising a son with multiple disabilities, and I admired her very much. She said in response, "I'm sure that God will give you the strength to deal with any situation in your marriage when it comes." I believed her, and I guess I rode on the coattails of her faith until I had my own.

Before my husband and I got married, while we were in the "discussion" stage, I asked him if he was apprehensive about starting another family at sixty. He said "If I could have twenty years with you I would be happy." Somehow, I got it in my mind that twenty years was all we were going to have, so each year was a countdown. But at ten years my attitude began to change, as I realized how blessed I was to have him and what a good fit we were. He was an excellent provider, a loving father and a good husband. He was always growing and changing as a person, even if he didn't appear to want to change. And he truly loved me. It was then that I began to cherish our time together, appreciating every day.

Marriage has been remarkable in many ways, but on a spiritual level, I realized that God showed his love for me through my husband. I often felt unlovable, particularly as I "outgrew" some old behaviors and coping mechanisms that no longer suited my lifestyle. I was developing self-knowledge, although slowly and painfully. It seemed like there was always another character defect—like a painful thorn in my flesh—to pull out, examine closely and throw away. But through it all, my husband loved me uncompromisingly, passionately and patiently. I started to understand that he was showing me the type of love that God has for me—consistent and without reservation. Although my husband occasionally became angry with me when I made bad choices or hurt him or others, his love never stopped. Eventually, I began to realize that his earthly love was only a microcosm of God's divine love. I started to glimpse God's enormous, unstoppable, pervasive love, and that all was truly well.

When I lost my connection with that love, I became fearful. Then I projected my dissatisfactions outward. In my journal I wrote about being upset with a good friend because I found her to be critical, upset with my family because I felt they weren't being supportive, upset with my co-workers because there were "unspiritual". Most of all, I became upset with myself when I was not living up to my own expectations. I have always struggled with perfectionism and have judged myself far more severely than I judge others. I am most miserable when I compare myself to others or to my idealized expectations of them. I am better when I practice acceptance of each situation as it arises and gratitude for all situations, but those are my "good days." When my son was coming home I had plenty of "bad days" because I had plenty of fear, as I was worrying about his re-entry into school and his ability to cope with the stresses there. In reality, we worked hard to get him the support he needed, and he did well when he returned, successfully completing his freshman year.

So here I was, enrolled in a new adventure with my own return to school, my older son back at home, my younger son doing well, our family intact, life moving forward. Yet off and on I was besieged by doubts and sadness, accompanied by frequent migraine headaches which I refused to let slow me down. In fact, it really aggravated me that an illness had the ability to control me. My refusal to give in to the headaches and simply rest and heal when they came probably made them last longer. But they made me so angry! I could not figure out what was causing them, other than "stress." How was I supposed to get the stress out of my life? Through the years I have changed my lifestyle to take better care of myself, but the headaches have persisted. I continue to attempt to identify triggers, slow down my activities and move toward healing.

****

My progression through graduate school seemed to be moving quickly: I finished a second class in June by enrolling in a summer session. Financially, ways to pay for the classes came along as needed, another sign that I was on the right track. Abba House was always on my mind, and I was able to visit often, even if only for a few hours at a time; it was nice to connect with the peace and solitude. I always felt the presence of God when I was there. In June, I went to Abba House for an afternoon to reflect, when our son once again started refusing to attend church, and my husband did not want to force him. I felt strongly that our son should go to church and was disappointed that my husband did not agree. Somehow, even if we fought to get there on Sunday morning, things were always better at home after we returned from Mass. It was like we absorbed grace just by being in the Lord's house. Of course, I was afraid. So I went to Abba House to find my courage, as well as feel my feelings. It was safe enough to cry there. I read a book that Father Simon had given me, an "Elf Help" book that said "if you have tears, cry."

In August, I returned to Abba House for a full weekend. I was exhausted and slept twenty-two of the forty-eight hours I was there, only to find out later that I had a bladder infection. I didn't want to meet with Sister Libby while I was there because I was edgy and found her frequent "discussions" with Sister Mary Gen irritating. I felt like I was around enough arguing and dissension at home. I did not realize that Sister Libby's health was beginning to fail.

In spite of the good chunk of time I spent sleeping that weekend, I returned home with some new tools in my spiritual toolbox. I had focused on the Letter to James, particularly restraint of pen and tongue, and reflected on ways I could apply that principle at home. I also spent some time reflecting on the phrase "God loves a cheerful giver," and vowed to use that phrase as a mantra in my dealings with my family.

These tools came in handy during August, when we adopted our first family dog: a three year old rescued Greyhound named Eevee. She was a beautiful black dog with as many "issues" as we had. She was not approachable while lying down and would snap at anyone who tried to touch her when she was not standing (Greyhounds rarely sit.) We learned that, very occasionally, Greyhounds develop territorial issues, since they are crated during most of their lives on the racetracks and their crates are their territory. We loved Eevee, but between her stringent boundaries and my son's lack of boundaries, my stress level when they were together was greatly increased. At least daily, he would try to pet her when she was lying down and she usually growled. Then we would reprimand him in an attempt to make him stop, which he usually ignored. She would continue to growl, our voices would get louder, and the exchange would end either with her snapping or us yelling. I would like to say she taught us a lot about boundaries, but most of the time it felt like she was just another thing to tell my son not to do.

Shortly after Eevee joined us at home, we boarded her with a family of Greyhound owners for a week in late August, to head out for our annual family vacation at Hampton Beach. Our time at the beach was always special, as the sea brings out the best in us. We sat on the beach for hours, ate lobster several evenings, enjoyed the arcades and fireworks with the kids. The only downside was that we missed Eevee. But she was happy to see us when we returned, and we brought her home and began the process of attempting to blend her into our family.

In September of that year, I turned forty, which I heard was going to be a milestone, but felt like more of a blip on my radar. I was excited to be starting a new career, and felt intellectually stimulated by my coursework. I was aging physically, which I found a bit sad, because I did not have the time or energy to maintain the figure I have been proud of my entire life. But I guess letting go of some of that pride was a good thing. Time that I previously had spent exercising was now spent reading, studying or writing papers.

When my sons and I returned to school that same month, I found the schedule challenging. I was working my usual three days per week, and we had regular meetings with the high school teachers and counselors to keep a watchful eye on our older son. The research class in the fall was very difficult and was a stretch for me in many ways I was discovering that graduate studies involved a lot of cooperative group work to prepare us for the group care model that was so prevalent in Special Education. However, it was very different from my undergraduate work of twenty years earlier.

At home, there seemed to be a lot more bickering, particularly between my husband and older son, so we found a new family therapist through one of the priests at our church. I did not like this therapist, but my family seemed to respect him, and at least we were all sitting together in a room and trying to talk about things that were bothering us. We had a great willingness as a family to work out our problems together. So, although I felt like the sessions didn't help me much, I was grateful that we were trying.

As we approached the holidays, I looked for the good in every situation. I wrote a poem in my prayer journal.

> God of light
> I watch for you this morning.
> The candle I lit for you dances,
> and I think of David dancing before the Ark.
> He was alive with your love.

Some days I feel like that;
other days I feel tired, like today.
So many responsibilities in this life.
Even the dog wants my attention.

God help me to keep watching for you today
and to see you in all the demands of my life.
More opportunities to love you through them.
More chances to pay back the favors you've given.
More lights dancing in my life,
dancing before the Ark of your love.

There was plenty of wonderful family time during the holidays. My brother's daughters stayed with us for several days, which was a lot of fun. I always enjoyed being with my nieces. They were real "girl-y" girls, and I loved watching them play dress up and perform skits. I even got to play Barbies with them, which was great! In fact, that is one of our fondest memories of their visits: playing with the Barbie dolls. We would play in the spare room where they slept and laugh so hard at the things we made our dolls do; I remember falling off the bed once with laughter. I also had the first of what were to become annual family Christmas parties, inviting my aunts and uncles and parents and brother's family. Those parties became precious milestones each year, as we came together at Christmas.

ABBA HOUSE—PUBLIC EVENTS

Let your light so shine before all, that they may see your good works and glorify your Father in heaven. Matthew 5:26

Through the years, Abba House hosted a number of public events in large venues that often drew sizable audiences. These events reflected the Sisters' deep beliefs in the movement from prayer to action. The foundress of their Society, Saint Madeline Sophie Barat, summarized this vital aspect of the RSCJ mission as a reflection of the Easter dawn encounter between Mary Magdalene and Jesus.

> There is the spirit of the Society. Our first movement is to linger at the feet of the Master: that is the contemplative life, that is what we must do in prayer. But it is then that Jesus says to us: "Go, tell my brothers." Mary becomes an apostle. Why can we not say to the whole universe: "Know his Heart?"
>
> The Society of the Sacred Heart: History of a Spirit,
> Margaret Williams, RSCJ, p. 302

The first Abba House public event was in the fall of 1981 on the occasion of the House's tenth anniversary. It featured Brother David Steindl-Rast OSB, who had been instrumental in the start of Abba House through his interactions with Sister Libby at Mount Saviour Monastery, making him a fitting choice for a speaker. He was also a noted author and speaker, hermit, monk, doctor of experimental psychology and student of Zen Buddhism. The event was held at the Mercy High School auditorium in Albany, and consisted of two presentations on prayer. One was titled "Prayer: Moving toward the center—How we relate to God" and the other was called "Prayer: Moving out from the center—How we reach out to others."

> "You find meaning when you open yourself, get quiet and take a grateful attitude. Sometimes, we might think we can go on for a while without meaning in our lives, but sooner or later comes a time when we know we have to find it."
>
> Brother David Steindl-Rast,
> Albany Times Union, 1982.

Brother David's talk was one part of a three-pronged celebration for Abba House's tenth anniversary. In recognition of their burgeoning ecumenical charism, another part was an anniversary dinner at the Albany Polish Community Center in late October and featured bishops from both the Roman Catholic and Episcopalian dioceses as after-dinner speakers. The event doubled as a fund-raiser, since "friends" who were unable to attend were encouraged to purchase tickets to assist the House financially. A flyer from the celebration stated that Abba House had served over 5000 guests in its ten years of operation from 1971 to 1981. Finally, the Sisters invited all Friends and the general public to an Open House during one Sunday afternoon in November.

In November of 1982, Abba House sponsored a public event featuring Dr. Robert Muller, Assistant Secretary General of the United Nations. Dr. Muller, also referred to as the "Prophet of Hope" and the "U.N. Philosopher," spoke on "Global Spirituality: Beacon of Hope for the Nations, How You Can Make a Difference." The ecumenical panel of respondents at the event featured Rev. Stephen Ayres, Dr. S.R. Swaminathan, Rev. Thomas Phelan, and Mrs. Mary Reed Newland. The event was held at Bishop Maginn High School in Albany and co-sponsored by the Peace and Justice Commission of the Roman Catholic Diocese of Albany, the Peace Commission of the Episcopal Diocese of Albany, and Walt Chura's Simple Gifts Bookstore.

In December of 1983, the Abba Community hosted their largest public event when they sponsored a talk by Bishop Thomas J. Gumbleton, Auxiliary Bishop of Detroit, and President of the American Section of Pax Christi and Bread for the World. Bishop Gumbleton was also the Co-Author of the American Bishops' Pastoral Letter on War and Peace. The topic of Bishop Gumbleton's talk was "Peace Patterns—Prayer, Justice, Non-Violence." The event was co-sponsored by the Albany Diocesan Chapter of Pax Christi and the Albany Chapter of Bread for the World. The event was held at the Bishop Maginn High School auditorium in Albany and drew over 500 people. Sister Mary Gen recalled Bishop Howard Hubbard's comment about the attendance: "It was amazing how many people came!"

Several of the Abba House events were co-sponsored by the Albany Chapter of Pax Christi, the Catholic peace organization originally founded in France in 1945. The founders of Pax Christi came together to pray for peace in in the aftermath of two world wars in which French and German Catholics had killed one another by the millions, in spite of their belief in the same faith and celebration of the same Eucharist. They met to pray for forgiveness, reconciliation, and the peace of Christ. Pax Christi chapters have sprung up around the world to pray and work for peace through prayer, study and action. According to their website, chapters exist in over thirty countries, with a growing presence in Latin America and Africa.

> "Contemplative prayer rises by divine grace where there is total disarmament of the heart, and unfolds in an experience of love which is the moving force of peace."
>
> American Bishops' Pastoral Letter on War and Peace.

In March of 1984 the Sisters held a smaller event with a big name when they offered a series of talks by Jesuit priest and peace activist Dan Berrigan at Abba House. Once again, the event was co-sponsored by the peace organization Pax Christi. A 1984 article in The Evangelist by Sally Maloy described the event, which consisted of three talks, each of which lasted approximately one hour, followed by times of quiet prayer and then group discussion. The author, who was acquainted with Father Berrigan's anti-war activities, admitted that she was unimpressed with his actions that "left behind spilt blood, burnt draft cards and dented warheads." She seemed surprised to learn that Father Berrigan had a gentle, quiet side and that he spoke "about the peace movement as a work of healing and forgiveness." His Scripture-based talks focused on Jesus' healing works as being both "public and provocative." Father Berrigan demonstrated humility in admitting a lack of answers to some of the questions asked, and sometimes responded with an effective use of silence. His message of peace, prayer and healing was well received at Abba House.

In May of 1984, Abba Community offered a Peace and Justice Colloquium with Sister Ann E. Chester, IHM, one of the founders of the House of Prayer Movement. The event spanned three days and was titled "The Process of Integrating Spirituality and Action for Justice." It featured several components, including social analysis, theological reflection and pastoral planning, concluding with a commitment liturgy.

In October of 1984, Abba House and Barry House co-sponsored a public event that was also an ecumenical dialogue: "Monks of a Different Cloth—How They Experience the Cross and the Resurrection in Christian Unity." The speakers were Reverend Douglas Brown OHC (Episcopal Order of the Holy Cross, which was the same order to which Sister Mary Gen's father had belonged) and Reverend Charles Murphy SA (Society of the Atonement, Saranac Lake, New York). The event was held at Our Lady of Mercy Parish Center in Colonie. The flyer promoted the event as a "a celebration of the 25th anniversary of Barry House and of the warm friendship between Abba House and Barry House."

The following year, Abba House sponsored another public event, a lecture by Reverend Thomas F. Stransky CSP, a Paulist priest and active ecumenist. At that time, Father Stransky's ecumenical credentials were already impressive, including his role as a Consultor and founding staff member of the Vatican Secretariat for Promoting Christian Unity, as well as his membership on the Joint Working Group for the World Council of Churches and the Roman Catholic Church. In addition to Father Stransky's talk on "God's Truth and Love—How Far Do They Reach? Ecumenism and Evangelization," the event featured the following panel of respondents and was chaired by Reverend James Kane, Ecumenical Officer of the Roman Catholic Diocese.

- Reverend Joyce S. Giles, Executive Director, Capital Area Council of Churches
- Mr. Joseph Powers, Roman Catholic Layman and Ecumenist
- Reverend James J. Reid, Executive Director, Christians United in Mission

The event was endorsed by a number of local groups that were actively ecumenical, including the Ecumenical Commission of the Episcopal Diocese, the Ecumenical Commission of the Roman Catholic Diocese, the Ecumenical Commission of the Lutheran Diocese, the Capital Area Council of Churches, and Christians United in Mission. Bishop Howard Hubbard remembered Reverend Stransky's talk at the 1985 Abba House gathering as energizing and very timely for what was happening in the Capital District ecumenical community at that time. The Abba House September 3, 1985 Letter to Friends stated that the program was planned to "enrich the work on Evangelization being carried out in RENEW all over the diocese." The RENEW movement included small groups within parish communities across the Diocese that gathered regularly to pray, read Scripture and provide fellowship.

The theme of the Abba House twentieth anniversary was gratitude. In September of 1991, the annual letter excitedly announced the celebration of the anniversary. Events were planned, including two days of prayer, talks and celebration at St. Vincent de Paul Church in Albany. Prayer and liturgies were to be celebrated by Bishop Howard J. Hubbard of the Roman Catholic diocese and Bishop David Ball of the Episcopal Diocese. Brother David Steindl-Rast, OSB returned for the twentieth anniversary celebration. He gave two talks at St. Vincent de Paul Church. The first was on the topic "Thanksgiving as a Form of Prayer" and was preceded by evening prayer presided over by Bishop David S Ball,

Bishop of the Episcopal Diocese of Albany. The second evening Brother David spoke about "Prayer in the Twenty-First Century." His talk was preceded by a period of quiet reflection with Taize music, and followed with Eucharist celebrated by Bishop Howard Hubbard with Father Paul Roman as the homilist.

In keeping with the topic of gratitude, the Albany Times Union published a Letter to the Editor from the Sisters in the fall of 1990.

> We, the staff of Abba House of Prayer, wish to express, through *The Times Union*, our deep gratitude to the many good people in the Capital area who support the spiritual ministry of this house with their generous contributions of money and other diverse services.
>
> Now heading toward our 20th anniversary in 1991, we reflect with thanksgiving how we came here in 1971, having very little knowledge of the area. Over this span of years, we have experienced much loving interest and support, without which our work would not have been possible. Many of these persons frequent Abba House, but we also receive generous donations from the civic and business community, which contains many open hearts and purses. Your own religion editors and staff writers, especially Ray Pitlyk and Grace O'Connor, have also been most helpful with publicity.
>
> To us, all this is a great sign of hope in a somewhat materialistic culture. God's blessing be upon all of us in 1991.
>
> Sister Elizabeth Hoye
> Sister Mary Smyth

As a demonstration of gratitude to past and present Board members, Sisters Libby and Mary Gen invited them and their spouses to be their guests at a private dinner of thanksgiving at the Chariot Restaurant in Guilderland. They aptly used a quote from Brother David's book Gratefulness, the Heart of Prayer on their flyer for the event: "Living by the Word of God means feeding on it, being nourished by it, eating, drinking and assimilating that Word. The image of food and drink is always closely associated with living by the Word."

Brother David's presence in Albany for the event was noted by a lengthy article/interview in the Evangelist, in which he gave the House of Prayer movement credit for reviving the Catholic Church's sense of prayer as contemplation, bridging the distance between religious and lay lifestyles and paving the way for new ideas about Christian living and community. By bringing religious sisters into neighborhoods such as Western Avenue in Albany where Abba House was located, the House of Prayer movement turned nuns into neighbors. Houses of prayer made experiences of communion with God accessible to the layperson.

Brother David also spoke about the movement of certain aspects of Eastern spirituality into the Catholic church, during a time when many aspects of the Church had become mechanical and authoritative. Eastern spirituality brought the recognition that every person is a special kind of mystic, so mysticism was not to be reserved for only those in religious life. An excerpt from the article follows.

> **Question:** After 20 years in the House of Prayer movement, what have we learned about prayer? What is prayer?
>
> **Brother David:** Prayer is the cultivation of the Divine Life within us. The Divine Life is always there within us from birth. According to the creation account in the Old Testament, we are creatures who, from the first moment, from our first breath, are alive with God's own life. And prayer is the cultivation of this life.
>
> Thomas Merton—who was very much at the root of this House of Prayer movement, although in an indirect way—said: "The spiritual life isn't just a long journey where you put one step in front of the other. The spiritual life consists of opening your eyes and realizing that you are already there." Prayer is the cultivation of the awareness that you are already there.

> Prayer in the full sense is simply the overflow—praise, blessing, thanksgiving, petition—all flowing out of this overwhelming joy of the Divine Life being already in us.

Sister Ann Chester, IHM also attended the 20th anniversary, celebrating one of the country's longest-running houses of prayer.

In 1996 the Sisters celebrated 25 years of ministry with public talks by their guest speaker Father Raymond Brown, SS (Society of St. Sulspice). Father Brown was a noted Catholic Scripture scholar and theologian, member of the Faith and Order Commission of the World Council of Churches from 1968 to 1993 and member of several national and international ecumenical dialogue groups. Father Brown held four earned degrees and twenty-six honorary doctorates, was the author of twenty-five books on the Bible, and served as a professor at numerous colleges in the United States and abroad.

So it was quite a coup for the Sisters to secure him as a speaker at their silver anniversary event. His topics for the evening were "A Half-Century of Catholic Biblical Scholarship and the Future" and "The Gospels—How are We to Read Them?" The event, held at St. Vincent de Paul Church, drew over 400 people. In his talks, Father Brown emphasized the importance of focusing on the Gospels themselves rather than the historical Jesus and popular scholarly reconstructions.

On the Lighter Side: excerpt from a 1996 issue of Albany area weekly entertainment newspaper, the "Metroland:"

Best Religious Building We Hope Isn't What It Sounds Like
ABBA House of Prayer
647 Western Ave., Albany
Friday night and the lights are gray...
Looking out for a place to pray...ouch.

My House—Supported on All Sides

In spite of the heightened anxiety around Y2K—the year 2000—everyone made it through without any nasty technological or Armageddon-like incidents, including my own little family. What a build-up there was to that New Year! It was likely that the attention to the possible technological ramifications of the transition was part of the reason we had little actual fallout. At the same time, I realized that the media in our country has enormous power to produce emotion and reaction in our culture, demonstrated by the high level of anxiety many people expressed as they stocked their homes with water bottles, food and flashlights in preparation for something awful to happen. I found it quite startling. In my own family, we celebrated with sparkling juice, party hats, noisemakers and streamers. Photos of my sons and husband blowing their horns at midnight on New Year's Eve became my favorite pictures for a long time!

At the beginning of January I retreated to Abba House for a few days. I was very tired physically, and got a migraine while on retreat. During spiritual direction with Sister Libby I wanted to talk about the problems I was having controlling my eating, but she zeroed in on my exhaustion. We talked about my hectic schedule, and she suggested I speak with my husband about it. At that time, I was in the midst of a year-long assistantship which was paying the tuition for my classes in graduate school, but was also adding another ten hours per week away from home. I had been afraid of admitting to my husband that I was struggling with the schedule because I knew he was not completely content with my decision to leave my safe and secure New York State job to venture out into a new career. But Sister Libby, ever the practical advisor, pointed out that the schedule was making me sick, and I needed to ask for help.

I discussed the issue with my husband and he conceded that my schedule was overly full. I reduced my work schedule from three days per week to one, which relieved a lot of my stress. I was able to enjoy the assistantship, which consisted of meeting with undergraduate students in the School of Social Welfare and helping them hone their writing skills. I had my own "office" at the school, which I decorated to my own taste and greatly enjoyed. When I didn't have appointments, I was able to study in my quiet office and feel rested, comfortable and at peace. When I did have appointments, I got to meet lovely people who were eager for assistance and very pleasant.

****

In what appeared to me as very strange timing, I was offered a promotion at work. I turned it down without giving it much serious consideration, since I was in the process of leaving my position with New York State and beginning a new career. Once again, I felt like God used the situation to work on my pride: after I refused the promotion, I overheard my co-workers verbally lusting after a promotion. I wanted to boast about being offered one and turning it down but couldn't, because I had promised not to talk about the offer due to the fact that it was tied into some reorganization that was not yet general knowledge. I also knew that I was not ready to supervise others; I had far too many of my own issues that required attention before I would be able to deal with others' issues via the supervision process.

At the same time, there was plenty going on in my prayer life. My older son was making some bad choices, we were confronting him, which made him angry, and he was taking that anger on the family. I did not like the way I was yelling at him, so I prayed and read the Bible, in search of answers. I looked for personalities I could identify with, such as David in the Old Testament, who was passionate and human. His honest repentance for his faults and his acceptance of God's forgiveness was inspiring. Despite all of his foibles, David was a man after God's own heart. I really wanted that kind of connection with God. I also seized on passages like Hebrews 8:18 "Because He Himself was tested through what he suffered, he is able to help those who are being tested." As I struggled with my overeating, my anger at home and my pride at work, I found comfort in the assurance that Jesus was human, too. I was also strengthened when I read about Him going out into new territories to do new work, stepping away from familiar ground and out toward new ventures. In my work life, I felt like I was leaving a place of familiarity and moving into a field where I often felt at a loss. It was risky and scary. But I also knew my career change was a part of my spiritual journey, and I was consulting God every step of the way.

The people in my life were another source of strength, and I was always amazed at the connections our family made as we asked for help in dealing with our various issues. Many of those connections were deeply satisfying, though occasionally they were unsettling, like the therapist we were seeing at the time for family therapy. I am grateful that I didn't simply discount this therapist because I took a personal dislike to him. If I had, I would have missed the lessons learned during our time together. It was probably because I was uncomfortable with him that my character defects—the ones that contributed the most to our family unrest—were front and center during our sessions together. So I was able to recognize the behaviors I needed to be mindful of, pray about and work on. I was learning that people and situations I find "difficult" are usually my greatest teachers.

My friends were a real blessing, too. When I needed guidance, comfort or solace, I knew I could turn to them. I remember a negative comment a co-worker made about me during a meeting. I took my pain to God and laid it on the altar (figuratively) during noon Mass one day. And after the Mass, I shared it with a friend I met there. She acknowledged the real hurt I was feeling and compared it to the hurt Jesus must have felt when the same people who praised him as the Messiah on Sunday were responsible for his being nailed to the cross on Friday. I was grateful to her for showing me how to identify with Jesus in my daily life. At other times, friends helped me by letting me help them. A friend from my past called me one day, distraught because her son had gotten into some trouble. As a result of my own experiences, I was able to be present, compassionate and resourceful. By being on both the giving and receiving end of compassionate care, I started to gain a deeper understanding of how we bless others when we allow them to minister to us.

We had given up fighting the church battle with our older son, so my husband and I went to Sunday Mass each week with just our younger son. One Sunday we were welcoming a new member into the church through the Rite of Christian Initiation (RCIA). Our faith community witnessed the RCIA rituals during Sunday Mass, which was encouraging to both the candidate and the community. As part of the rite this particular week, the priest and the candidate's sponsor blessed the young man, on his eyes so he could see the truth, his ears so he could hear the Gospel, and the other senses as well. Our younger son leaned over to me and whispered, "I wish somebody would bless my brother like that."

By March, our older son was refusing to get out of bed in the morning, and it became a daily ordeal for me to attempt to try to convince him to go to school. Some days I had no patience and did a lot of yelling and threatening. Other days I could coax him out. More than half of the time he missed the bus, so I would drive him to school. On the days he did not get up, I knew we would come home from work at the end of the day and find him planted in front of the television or computer, sullen and belligerent if we attempted to get him to do anything productive or share the space with the rest of the family. Knowing what I was returning home to at the end of the day weighed heavily on my mind while I was at work, distracting and depressing me. He was also becoming increasingly angry and violent around the house, and we called the police several times at the suggestion of the professionals we were working with. I was consumed with anxiety because it seemed like we were heading down the same road we had already traveled, which had led to his placement in a residential treatment facility two years before. We continued to look for treatment options—programs, medications, professionals—to help him, but by now he was noncompliant. He had taken so many different medications he probably felt there was no use taking any more. If he was prescribed something and I brought it to him, he pretended to take it and I would find it later under a cushion or in a tissue. We also discovered he was experimenting with other substances, doing his own version of self-medicating.

Despite, or maybe because of, all of this chaos, my spiritual growth continued. I included this quote from a spiritual writer who was a teacher of Centering Prayer, Thomas Keating, in my spiritual journal: "The spiritual journey is initiated when we become aware that our ordinary psychological consciousness is dominated by the false self with its programs for happiness and over-identification with our cultural conditioning." In my journal I wrote about going to the drugstore to fill a prescription to treat a bout of bronchitis and a sinus infection:

> I was drawn to a display for barrettes: they were so pretty! I had to be really strong to resist buying them. I thought of my husband's admonishment to resist impulse buying because of my reduced wages, but after reading this passage today I see that there is a still deeper meaning: cultural conditioning. How deeply my belief goes that ***things*** will make me better. It's no wonder I've been on a quest to make more money my whole life! It's no wonder it has been such a struggle to go back to school and change careers. I heard a woman say the other day that if she felt bad she could always go out and buy some shoes. I identified so deeply with that. Now I see how so much of this is at the center of my being. It must be rooted out and looked at. Keating says that is done with Centering Prayer.

My prayers were cries from the heart. On Ash Wednesday, I prayed to make a good Lent. My husband and I decided to make an effort to regularly kneel and pray a decade of the Rosary together. I asked God for peace in my family. I prayed for strength and courage to not project what the future might hold: it was too easy to slip into fear and discouragement about the bad choices I was seeing my son make almost daily. I was so frightened. I could not bear the thought of our family being torn apart again, so I prayed for help to keep us together.

The more I prayed, the more God answered my prayers. My older son had several teachers at school who were real blessings. His resource room teacher was also his soccer coach, so they were able to connect in a few different ways, and he became an important part of my support system. He gave me a lot of telephone time, encouraging me when I was frustrated with my inability to enforce my son's school attendance. Although I didn't even address the homework issue since my son hadn't done homework in years, I maintained that any day he did some work in school was a good day. Another teacher appealed to my son's creative side and helped him relate to and connect with his peers. This teacher ran a talent show at the school: he was very funny, allowing himself to be on the receiving end of the students' antics.

My prayers were also answered through the therapist I found to help my younger son deal with his anxiety. Because he was witnessing his brother's angry and occasionally violent outbursts, he was having difficulty sleeping at night. I asked some of the professionals we were utilizing for recommendations to a therapist who worked well with younger children, and we found a social worker who was gentle, creative and "kid-friendly." She helped my younger son to vocalize his fears and develop coping mechanisms for the scary times.

Another huge answer to a problem that had been plaguing me for many years was my discovery of a Bible based weight loss program to help me deal with my tendency to overeat when tired or stressed. Through this program I learned that I didn't have to diet anymore, that it is wiser to pay attention to empty and full feelings than to use popular and expensive weight loss programs emphasizing portion control. I realized that I never kept lost weight off and that I was keeping those companies in business by not learning how to eat in a healthy way. This program worked for me because it was Bible based, stressing that we should go to God to meet our needs rather than run to the refrigerator. I embraced this program, first by reading the books and implementing as much as I could on my own and later by joining a formal group at a local church. At the time this program helped me immensely and was truly an answer to my prayers. I dove even more deeply into the Word and addressed an issue that had been taking up far too much of my time and energy.

Creativity blossomed in an unexpected area when my nighttime dreams started to be more meaningful. One night, I had a dream about a girl I was working with through my assistantship. She was a lovely girl who had transferred from a community college and was the most eager-to-learn student I worked with. She took every suggestion I made and tried to apply everything she learned in her subsequent writing assignments. Her advisor/teacher, who was also my supervisor, noticed the difference as a result of our work together. In my dream, I delivered her baby, which was a joyous experience for both of us, even though in "real life" she was not pregnant. Actually, I was assisting in her birth as a communicator, which was also a joyous experience. Dreams can be such wonderful reflections of the things in life that really matter. I believe that God truly can speak to me through my dreams. That particular dream about my student affirmed my abilities as a teacher, writer and mentor.

Several weeks later I wrote this poem about Centering Prayer.

My Lord looks for me.
He peers around the corner
like a child playing peek,
then darts away so quickly.
His laughter bounces off the wall down the hall.

My Lord waits for me.
Sometimes the chair rocks gently
when I enter the quiet room.
He has been waiting there for me.
I ease into his arms
and we rock.

My Lord lives in me.
He loves me with a passion
that carries me away from myself
and brings me to him.
He gathers the scattered light of my soul
and I heal.

Not surprisingly, I had several particularly vicious migraine headaches as I moved toward the end of another semester of graduate school—always stressful—and dealt with the truancy issues at home. At the same time, I was also attempting to stop using food—particularly sweets—for comfort. When I went into self-flagellating mode as I tried to apply the new "Godly" eating principles I was learning about, I was successful for a few days, then reverted to overeating when there was a tough time at home. Instead of recognizing the gains in my behavior modification, I focused on the failures. Then I would become depressed and centered on myself and another headache would come. It was a difficult time.

The negativity was broken by the celebration of our younger son's First Eucharist, a very special day for several reasons. It was a unifying event for the family: my stepdaughter brought her children to the church and then to our house for a little get-together. My mother and father brought my niece. And my older son came to church with us, which he hadn't done in a long time. In preparation for First Eucharist, I had asked my son's teacher at his Catholic school if I could visit the class a few times and play "Bible Bingo" with the students, a game I had played with several of my religious education classes. Because of my time with my son's class, I felt very connected to a number of the students. It was a blessed day.

On Mother's Day I had a pity party! I was resentful because my husband didn't take the boys shopping to get me anything: I compared that to the efforts I expended to make Father's Day special for him. Nursing that resentment was not a good choice, emotionally or spiritually. A grateful heart is a happy heart: I was not happy!

Up and down, up and down: from day to day my mood went from elated to depressed. Even though the tough times were very hard, they pushed me closer to God. I wrote in my journal:

> O Lord, I fling this burden at your feet. Please take it. I am so tired of handling this situation without you. You take it today. Relieve me of my resentments. Please heal my anger. Let me be at peace with this. I love you, Lord,

> and I know you can fix anything. Please fix my family. To me, it seems broken. If it isn't, please help me to see that. Lately my eyes are cloudy and my heart is confused. I only see the bad and the broken. I focus on the negative. Please help me to see the good things.

A few weeks after writing that I was blessed with a weekend retreat in the Adirondacks with my church women friends. Once again, we went to one of the women's camps and had a wonderful time. I particularly enjoyed the nightly bonfire, when we passed around a talking stick and told of the qualities that we most admired in each other. I was greatly encouraged by the comments the women made, because I respected them. After years of feeling "less than" others, I was finally able to hear and take in compliments when they said that I was greatly admired, that I was a loyal and true friend, and that it was evident I was deeply loved by God. The retreat refreshed and reinvigorated me.

In June, I re-committed to daily Centering Prayer, having drifted from it as I became enmeshed in the daily drama of trying to get my older son to school. I decided to let the proverbial chips fall, since he was beyond saving from the consequences of his actions: he was headed toward summer school. Family therapy was kicking up a lot of "stuff" that needed healing in me regarding my fears about the future and my inability to control others' choices, which elevated my insecurities around my graduate work. I knew that Centering Prayer was a great place to take these hurting parts of myself.

A good thing that came out of our family therapy was our consciousness-raising around the quantity of television we watched. We agreed that for the summer we would turn off all the televisions in the house (we had several) from noon to six pm each day. Although this was difficult at times, there were great rewards. We talked to each other more. The kids found alternative things to do, like reading, drawing, and playing outside. It was quieter.

The summer passed relatively smoothly. I was still enrolled in the Bible based weight loss class that helped me to deal with my habits of overeating while leading me more deeply into the Bible. Because I was only working one day each week, I had more time to spend with the family. The boys were ushers in a family friend's wedding: we had a lot of fun and made a great memory. We dealt with family issues such as my father's bout with cancer in a positive way, coming together to talk about it and share our fears and hopes. We enjoyed a week at the beach together. There was less stress in the house because we did not have to fight the daily school battle. The few weeks of summer school my son had to attend were late enough in the morning and short enough in both length and duration that we got through them relatively unscathed.

In September of 2000, the stress picked up when school started again. I took a few days' retreat at Abba House when my son once again threatened violence in our home. I prayed and asked for wisdom and guidance. In the silence of the House I heard what I needed to hear: when I returned home I had to be quieter. A lot of what was going on at home had to do with my wanting peace in the house so desperately that I stuck my nose in everybody else's interactions. I did not let my husband discipline our older son, so my husband became increasingly frustrated. My son learned how to manipulate me, playing on my sympathies and convincing me to do things that my husband did not want me to do, such as buying things for him even when he was unable to follow our house rules. I really had trouble controlling my tongue, and it became clear on that retreat that I needed to. I certainly did not like the prescription God gave me on that retreat, but I returned home resolved to at least try to address it.

Underlying my verbosity at home was an urge to control what I was seeing as uncontrollable. Underlying that was fear, of course. I identified it as anger, but it went far deeper than that. I always hear that God never gives you more than you can handle: what I could deal with at that moment was to work on my character defect of anger. I wrote in my journal:

> God's gentle nudges encouraging me to work on my anger have come just in time. I see that I will need His grace through this conversion process, as my Lord works gently to lift this character defect from me. (Although, I have to admit, that at times it feels more like he is drilling it out of me without the aid of Novocain.)

I tried different ways of dealing with the angry attacks at home, by leaving the room or becoming silent. I measured how important things were before I spoke. I deferred to my husband more in decisions about the children. As a result, the household became a bit more peaceful and ran more smoothly.

In the fall, I finished my graduate coursework with my comprehensive exams, which were very challenging. I grappled with fear about my ability to be successful in my career change as I anticipated the start of student teaching in January. The anxiety kept me close to God. I prayed a lot about where I might be going, because it was all very confusing.

> Lord, I am positive this is where you want me to be because of the way things have gone in the past few years. Don't let me lose my heart now. This is like the crucial point for me, the point that I never really allowed myself to think of because I was afraid to. Let me feel your presence Lord. Give me a two-fold measure of your spirit.

About this time I adopted a prayer written by Thomas Merton as my own.

> My Lord God, I have no idea where I am going.
> I do not see the road ahead of me. I cannot know for certain where it will end.
> Nor do I really know myself, and the fact that I think I am following your will does not mean that I am actually doing so.
> But I believe that the desire to please you does in fact please you, and I hope that I have that desire in all that I am doing.
> And I know that if I do this, you will lead me by the right road although I may know nothing about it.
> Therefore I will trust you always.
> Though I may seem to be lost and in the shadow of death, I will not fear, for you are ever with me and you will never leave me to face my perils alone.

I posted this prayer on my refrigerator and prayed it often. It reminded me that as long as I put God's will before my own, all would be well. Even if I made what appeared to be a bad choice, if I did it with a good heart and maintained a true desire to be God's instrument, all would be well. I was learning that God was so much bigger than my choices or circumstances, and so I began to understand what Jesus meant when he stood condemned before the Romans: "Any power that you have comes from my Father in heaven." I was learning that it was all good, even if it didn't appear that way from the world's perspective.

So my gratitude increased exponentially as I moved into this new phase of my life. I was blessed by being willing to express that gratitude through my relationships with others. I wrote this poem for two of my good friends and shared it with them.

You bring to me your loving hearts,
your kind and gentle ways,
And so I see God's grace in you
in different precious ways.

The way you smile, the way you laugh,
brings lightness to my soul
So many times your healing joy
has once more made me whole.

Your prayerfulness is such a gift,
I'm so inspired to see
the way you trust our Father's ways
will bring what's meant to be.

Your loyalty to those you love,
another strength in you.
Through storms and tribulations
you stay steadfast and true.

My gift to you this day is small
in terms of worldly measure
Instead with words I thank you for
the gift of YOU I treasure.

So thank you both for all you are
And all you're yet to be.
Your prayers, your words, your joy, your love.
You are God's gift to me.

ABBA HOUSE CALENDARS

Each year the Abba House sisters gifted the Board members and close friends of the House with beautiful handmade calendars. Sister Mary Gen used original photography and the sisters collaborated on carefully selected Scripture quotes, themes and formats for the calendars. Following is a selection of a few of my favorites.

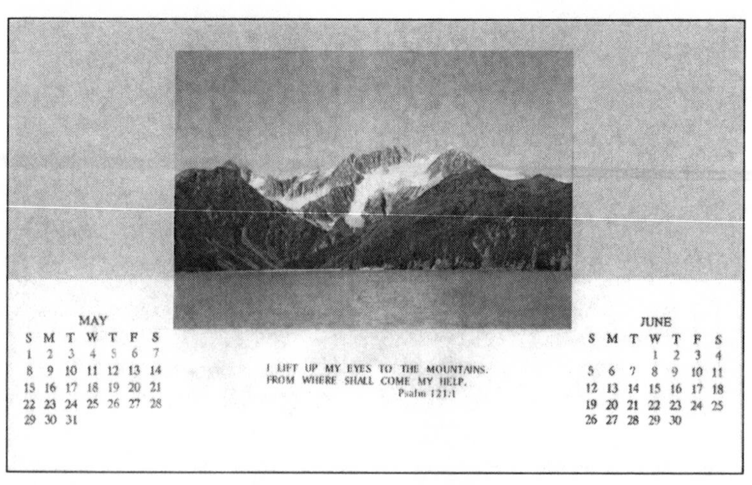

1994 Abba House Calendar

Pictures representing God's glory in the beautiful state of Alaska

1990 Abba House Calendar The Cloud of Unknowing: "Enter this Cloud and be at home in it."

S	M	T	W	T	F	S
					1	2
3	4	5	6	7	8	9
10	11	12	13	14	15	16
17	18	19	20	21	22	23
24	25	26	27	28	29	30
31						

1995 Abba House Calendar

Stained glass windows from churches in the Albany area

1998 Abba House Calendar
A Year of Peace and Calm
(photos from Catskill
Game Farm)

ON EITHER BANK OF THE RIVER WERE THE TREES OF LIFE. REV 22:2

JUNE

		1	2	3	4	5
6	7	8	9	10	11	12
13	14	15	16	17	18	19
20	21	22	23	24	25	26
27	28	29	30			

THE UPRIGHT WILL FLOURISH LIKE A PALM TREE. PSALM 92:12

DECEMBER

			1	2	3	4
5	6	7	8	9	10	11
12	13	14	15	16	17	18
19	20	21	22	23	24	25
26	27	28	29	30	31	

1999 Abba House Calendar
Trees

My House—Stepping Out in Faith

In December of 2000, convinced that my future was in teaching, I severed my ties with New York State. This was a great leap of faith for me, although it now seems like my husband could see the future more clearly than I could. During my seven years of teaching, whenever I became discouraged or weary, he would repeat "you can always go back to the State." And he was right; the State was always an option for me. I had done good work during my fourteen-year tenure and was well respected. While I was teaching, my former manager would periodically contact me to ask if I was interested in returning, so I knew that I always had a safety net. But when I left in 2000, I prepared to transfer my retirement accruals to the Teacher's Retirement System, fully believing that I would never return to State employment.

My office-mates gave me a lovely going away luncheon. My mother and my husband attended and several of the managers spoke about what a good worker I was and how much I would be missed. They commented that my future students were very lucky to have me as a teacher. There were many good wishes. When I was preparing for this farewell luncheon, I had written in my journal "Holy Spirit, give me the words to speak when it is my turn. I want to give God the glory and the praise for my ability to change careers at this point in my life." But when it was time for me to speak, I couldn't think of anything to say other than "thank you" and "I will miss you." My husband said I "did good." It was probably better that way. God always knows better than I do.

When I left my job, Father Simon, my friend from the Cathedral, gave me a beautiful hand painted icon of Jesus the Teacher. His friend had painted it with me in mind. Father Simon knew a lot about my personal and professional situation, so the painter probably knew what I was grappling with at home and where I was headed in my career. It is a beautiful icon that is still over my dresser so I can see it when I lie in bed. Jesus' gaze is steady and intense, as if He is looking into my soul.

When I began my student teaching in an elementary school Resource Room, I immediately became sick with a bad cold, which turned into bronchitis and then laryngitis. Once again there were blessings in the difficult times, as I observed how my inability to speak affected my family. It seemed that when I lost my voice my husband found his.

By now, our son was only attending school intermittently. It was ironic that I was entering the world of education as he was dropping out of school. We had almost given up fighting with him about attending school since it required a significant amount of energy every morning, and I needed my energy for the daily challenges of student teaching. He had also continued to self-medicate with alcohol and drugs, and I was very frustrated by the danger I knew he was in. One night, when I was full of frustration and anger, I told him to just go out and get drunk. My husband was shocked. Later he asked me how I would feel if our son did that, to which I replied "very guilty." One of my daily meditation books contained a quote from Jonathan Swift: "Whoever is out of patience is out of possession of his soul. Men must not turn into bees who kill themselves in stinging others." That is what I felt like I was doing when I lashed out in anger against my son. Fortunately, I had returned to individual therapy, so I was able to process these events with a professional instead of repeating them.

I was doing a great deal of work with my therapist, much of it focused around my relationship with my ex-husband. I realized that some of the anger I expressed toward my son was related to the guilt I felt over my relationship with his father. There were some major red flags around that man, and I ignored them all. I also ignored the advice of most of my friends and relatives to steer clear. Now that our son was a teenager and having so much trouble, it seemed almost like a Karmic "I told you so" from somebody out there (not God—I never believed that). Part of my therapy involved healing from post-traumatic stress disorder by using EMDR (eye movement desensitization and reprocessing). This fascinating practice allowed me to re-visit traumatic times in a non-threatening manner, enabling healing and closure around some of my past experiences, several of which included my ex-husband. This work and the talk therapy used with it brought a measure of peace I hadn't felt since my pre-teen years.

As we continued to deal with the challenges in our home, I stayed in prayer, communicating my hopes and fears to my Lord and looking for answers. I wrote in my prayer journal:

> You are always good to me. So many times you offer me blessings, but it is up to me to reach out my hands and take them. That is the way it is with relationships—the struggles and trials we have to go through in relationship with others are often hard and bruising. We are capable of hurting each other in so many ways. When we open our hearts to forgive and love each other we always encounter a wealth of rewards—an abundance of blessings, like in the passage where you talk about a good measure, pressed down and overflowing. I see that as so much of everything good poured in my lap. And I see myself laughing with joy at how blessings overflow in my life.
>
> Lord, I pray that I will always remain open to the joys of relationship. Let me not harden my heart at the pain inflicted by those who love me the most.
>
> My littlest blessing just came in...

More challenging situations came up at home, and we asked for more professional help. I focused on being grateful for many things: good health, an intact family, opportunities to do new and challenging things in my professional career, a living and growing relationship with God. At that time I had a good friend,

Forest, who has since gone to Heaven. Forest prayed a lot for me and my son, and his prayers gave me such hope. He had a deep, real faith in God and His power and goodness. One time I was telling him about the latest exploits and he shook his head and said, "How do you get Jesus into a person's life?" I said I didn't know, but I knew that Jesus was in my house. (That had been my theme at one of my Abba House presentations: "God is in the house!")

One of the things Forest told me was that God put us together in the first place, so He can put us back together if we are broken. I believed that then, and I am seeing it lived out as I write this, years later, as my son lives a fruitful, positive life. Recently in church the homilist said that as Catholic Christians we are people of the book and so when we are discouraged, we should go to the book to be encouraged by God's promises. And his promises are many and varying. He went over a few of them, and I found myself nodding, thinking about all of the difficult times we went through in our family. Some of God's promises are that we will be fruitful and contented and useful. When he said that God promises us our "heart's desires" my heart flip-flopped in my chest. For sitting at my left was my older son, back in church with us again. Having him worshiping in church next to me on Sunday was my "heart's desire" for many, many years. I felt truly blessed.

But in 2001, when we were in one of the tough times, the future seemed a long way off. It was hard to stay upbeat when we faced daily difficulties. And at times I was besieged with envy. I remember one Sunday sitting behind a friend of mine at church, watching her and her children. They were all present, and all appeared to be well-behaved and beautiful. My son was absent, ill and difficult to deal with. I wrote

> I still compare myself to others; I still say in my mind "you don't understand." I still mentally complain of how hard my days are, listing the litany of tiring and negative experiences. Lord, I need your help to carry these crosses gracefully. Sometimes I am so tempted to whine and complain and eat and smoke. You are really the only one who can help me.

We kept asking for help. We found an intensive adolescent outpatient program affiliated with a local hospital. Over the next year our son went into that program three times, managing to finish it the third time. Our home life was fraught with tension, anger, and recriminations. I had hoped that the outpatient program would help, but few of the challenging behaviors seemed to dissipate. If anything, he seemed to be getting more defiant and angry, probably because he was being confronted about his behavior by people outside as well as inside our home.

I fought with my tendency to react rather than act when faced with his anger. I desperately wanted to deal with these situations more peacefully, to be calm when faced with trouble. I knew that my angry reactions to his anger stemmed from the fear and panic I felt. I prayed and prayed for self-restraint. Most of my journal entries were filled with entreaties to God—to help me to react less, to send people to help us, that we would have a breakthrough of some sort. Every few days I felt spiritually fit and confident that my prayers would be answered, like on this day:

> Every day I come to your Word, and every day I am refreshed. I am renewed with hope that springs from you alone, for you are ever faithful and encouraging. Your love is constant and limitless, reflected on every single page. How could I face the things I see and feel each day without you? I would crumble in the midst of these trials and adversities. I would simply dissolve into the nothingness of my former sinful ways of coping. You teach me to stand fast, to wait on Your Word, to be patient and trusting that You know better than I do in all things. You give me hope.

In the midst of this, my oasis of peace—Abba House—appeared to be disintegrating. Sister Libby's health had been failing for some time, and she was also having episodes of mental confusion that worried Sister Mary Gen. In February, I went to Abba House to spend an afternoon with Sister Libby, knowing that she was not feeling well. She asked about my son, and I told her about the program he was enrolled in. She became agitated and yelled at me, telling me that nothing I was doing was working with him, that I should just wake up and accept that. I yelled back at her "I know that!!" I was deeply disturbed and shaking. She was not the same person I had known and loved for the past seven years. A few weeks later her deteriorating health led to her move from Abba House to the nursing unit at Kenwood.

In my family, my son's foray into drugs and alcohol led us to make some hard choices, some of which involved the legal system. Once again, we made several emergency calls to our local police department, who always did their best to be professional and helpful, with a touching gentleness. In retrospect, I see how blessed we were with and by those gentlemen, although it certainly didn't feel that way at the time.

Desperate for some measure of peace in the house, we took our son to Family Court. I prayed that God precede us into the courtroom and that the judge operate in wisdom. My prayers were answered. I remember us filing into the courtroom, after sitting for several hours in the waiting area. The judge read our case file and listened to the law guardian describe the events that had led up to our appearance. He looked up at us and asked us, "do you want your son out of your house? My husband answered, "No, your Honor, we just want him to take his medication." The judge made that requirement a condition of the order of protection that he issued, warning that if our son did not comply by taking his medication on a regular basis, he could be removed from our home. Although I was very grateful that our time in Court had provided us with some real authority that had teeth in it (because neither my husband or I had the strength to put our obviously ill and extremely naive seventeen year old son out in the street), I was exhausted. This process was draining emotionally and physically. And I was also still student teaching, working on completing a research project and raising another son at home. Sometimes I felt very cold and heartless. I did not like setting these firm boundaries—it felt foreign and mean and even cruel at times.

Once again, I had let go of my practice of daily Centering Prayer, even though I had figured out by now that it was a real grounding practice for me. But now that I reflect on everything that was happening at that time, I'm not surprised at my avoidance of Centering Prayer, especially since I was losing Sister Libby. I never skimped on the other time I spent with God—I was very disciplined about starting each day with Scripture reading, prayer and journaling. However, I had a very difficult time being consistent with meditation. No matter how many times I resolved to do it on a daily basis, I did not stick to it. I intuitively knew that my future professional success depended on my ability to commit to this invaluable practice. It would be several years before I developed a regular daily diet of prayer and meditation.

As I entered Holy Week in 2001, I was filled with remorse for not having made a "good Lent"—not sticking to my intentions at the beginning of that holy season. But I loved Holy Week. I tried to go to Triduum services (Holy Thursday, Good Friday and Holy Saturday) with my family every year. One of the most precious Holy Week memories I have is attending Good Friday service with my husband and younger son when he was about three years old. He had fallen asleep in my arms, so I sat in the pew with him instead of going up to the front of the church with the rest of the congregation to venerate the cross. I remember crying as I watched each person approach and kiss the cross. I had grown to know so many people at Our Lady of Mercy during the years I had been attending with my husband, that I knew a lot of their struggles as well as their joys, and thought about each of their own crosses as they approached.

I went to the Holy Week services. We planned on going to the Holy Saturday evening Mass as a family, so I bought new clothes for the boys (not much fun, really, since they didn't like to get dressed up). I always loved giving gifts to my children, so I had bought candy and little gifts for an Easter basket. My little boy and I colored eggs, which we always did. Then it was time to go to Mass on Saturday night, and my older son refused to get ready. So we went without him. I was so upset. I spent half the Mass being angry at him. I finally let the grace of the service settle in me and calm me down. When we returned home, he acted like nothing was wrong. In the night I awoke and smelled cigar smoke—once again he was breaking house rules by smoking in his room. I was so frustrated. I didn't give him an Easter basket, and he accepted that consequence quite gracefully. We went to my parents' house for Easter Sunday dinner, and all was well there. Once again, it felt like our family times were emotional rollercoasters. It was tiring.

After Easter, I enjoyed the daily Scripture readings that went with the Easter service. I wrote:

> Today we read of your appearance to the disciples. I am grateful for this time with your Word because it brings You so much closer to me. Without pausing to think about the mysteries of your life, death and resurrection, I would get completely caught up in my own little life, which I tend to do every time I get up from this table. I have this time with You before I get started, which grounds me in the reality of my faith. Thank you!

ABBA HOUSE—PERSONAL CONNECTIONS

"It wasn't just your average person who went to the House—the people it drew in were very unique. Abba House didn't have a lot of flash and flair, but it made quite a mark in Albany."
Terri Bronner

The interesting thing about researching this book was the constant uncovering of more activities the sisters were involved in, more groups that met at Abba House, more people whose lives were touched by the ministry of the House. Their influence was like a deep bottomless well that appeared small and limited to the casual observer but actually was abundantly rich and far-reaching.

One of the great gifts that the Abba House Sisters brought to many people was that of spiritual direction. They had remarkable teachers in the tradition of their religious community. The founder of the Society of the Sacred Heart, Sister Madeleine Sophie Barat, was highly respected for her gifts of spiritual direction. Evidence of the deeply personal relationships she developed through her direction of others exists in her letters, many of which are quoted in Sister Margaret Williams book on the Society. One follows.

> The calm and tranquility which you have enjoyed in your solitude and which still fill you have passed into my own soul...You have suffered so much and for so long a time,

> for so many years, that I am happy in the peace that floods your heart.

Like St. Madeleine Sophie, Sister Libby was truly present to those she directed, and I was blessed to be one of her own. She got to know us well, and we knew that she loved us. Justine Guernsey talked to me about having Sister Libby as her spiritual director, and as we talked, I felt like I was speaking with my spiritual sister. About Sister Libby, Justine said, "I called her my Yoda. She had a way about her. She would sit there and listen to me go on and on, never saying anything. I would wonder if she was even listening to me. Then she would come out with something really clear and powerful. She made things clear for me. She walked the walk with me."

A common theme that emerges when people talk about Abba House is how their time there helped them become comfortable with silence. Anne Snyder told me that one of the greatest gifts Abba House gave her was an appreciation of silent prayer, which is an important part of her life today. She started going to Abba House when her daughters were small and her life was noisy and busy: there was always radio, TV, children, people. She remembers being at an Abba House retreat day and being sent off by Sister Libby into the House for silent prayer. It was her first experience of being silent and alone on purpose. Anne said "Abba House taught me to be silent, present and in prayer. Thirty years later, I still go on a silent retreat each year." Justine Guernsey shared a similar experience that occurred when she was taking the Spirituality of Daily Life class. "They sent us off by ourselves to pray. That was an introduction to contemplation. It was the first time I had ever done anything like that. The first couple of times it nearly killed me: I was no good at waiting." The sisters used silence in their programs regularly. Justine remembers "there was extensive silence in some of the classes that could be challenging."

John and Diana Lynn Arber were on the Board at the same time I was. I remember being with them at the Kenwood event one evening in 2001 where we marked and celebrated the transition of the House's leadership from the two Sisters to Rosemary Sgroi RSM (Religious of the Sisters of Mercy). John and I remained close by Sister Libby for most of the evening. One of the guests at the event asked us if we were her family. When I was researching this book, John and I spoke by phone, as he and Diana Lynn now live in Canada. He told me that Diana Lynn had already been going to the House for awhile before he went for the first time. He attended a few retreats, a New Year's Eve's gathering, and a book study on C.S. Lewis. He said that "the House was always comforting and welcoming: we went for community, fellowship, and ease."

Helene Conroy said that Abba House was a "major portion" of her life. Helene was on the Board of Directors for many years, held several offices, attended numerous programs, and had personal and spiritual relationships with the two nuns. Helene credited the Sisters with her re-entry into the Roman Catholic Church. She had been away from the Church for about twenty-five years for a variety of reasons and wanted to go back. A friend told her about "Sister Libby and her progressive thinking" so she paid her a visit. Helene said "Abba House let me put my toes in the water slowly in returning to the church. I'm not sure it would have happened without them."

Kitt Jackson met the Sisters when she came to work for the Capital Area Council of Churches where they both served on the Board of Directors. An Abba House New Year's Eve event helped her to heal after her husband passed away: on her first New Year's Eve without him, she wanted to be among friends, not alone, but not "partying." She had always been struck by the fact that Abba House started the same year that she and her husband were married. According to Kitt, "that evening provided just the right atmosphere to move from a year of sorrow, pain and loss into a new year of peace and hope."

Walt Chura remembered Sister Libby and Mary Gen as "wonderful people." He got to know them when they visited his bookstore "Simple Gifts" during the 1970's at 813 Madison Avenue, which was in the Sisters' neighborhood. Walt had studied under Father Bill Shannon, who was the founder of the International Merton Society, and Sister Libby and Mary Gen asked if he could do a presentation on Merton at Abba House. Every few years they would ask him to come up with a theme for another presentation. He remembers them as "a perfect team: they were so different but they complimented each other so well." He has fond memories of sharing supper at the house before a scheduled program and talking with the Sisters about their spiritual journeys, movies they had seen, and other interesting topics.

> *I give thanks to my God at every remembrance of you, praying always with joy in my every prayer for all of you, because of your partnership for the Gospel, from the first day until now. Philippians 1:3*

In the late 1980's the Sisters began hosting an annual neighborhood picnic in their backyard each summer. They invited friends of the House and neighbors to "bring a dish to share and a chair for yourself" as noted on their flyers. The annual event became a popular occasion that dozens of neighbors, friends and Board members looked forward to each year. It was a chance to connect with friends and neighbors in a relaxed and friendly atmosphere. Carmela Richards, whose family owned the house next to Abba House, remembers a great turnout. She said, "the picnics were a good opportunity to meet people in the neighborhood that you usually didn't meet."

Abba House taught everyone who attended how to rest in God's love and care, which was manifested tangibly in the Sisters' love and care. During my time of spiritual direction with Sister Libby, she often focused on getting in touch with how much God loves us, stressing that there were many different ways to pray. That was a recurrent theme at Abba House, surfacing in a 1981 article in the *Schenectady Gazette* in which Sister Libby was quoted:

> Sister Hoye finds people often have trouble believing God loves them and this interferes with prayer. 'Some people don't believe God loves them just as they are so they believe they have to win his love by right actions,' she noted, pointing out that God loves people first and then motivates and assists to turn away from sin and selfishness—not the other way around.

Father Paul Roman said that “the Holy Spirit moved through the interaction of the people who came to the House.” He told story of a young Nigerian girl who he referred to the sisters for their assistance and friendship. Sister Libby took that responsibility very seriously. They stayed close to her through the years—there are pictures of her and her family visiting the House in the archives. That woman was Elizabeth Bassey, one of the founders of the Black Apostolate church in Albany. She has since passed away.

They were content to simply be God’s handmaids.
BJ Costello

MY HOUSE—TURNING CORNERS

As we moved toward May 2001 and my graduation, I reflected on my journey and prayed for the wisdom to make right choices in my job search. I had no idea where to apply for work or what grade level to teach. I often woke in the night and prayed for guidance. When I finished student teaching at a local elementary school, the district where I was working hired me as an aide for the balance of the school year. It was a struggle to be grateful for the $8 per hour they paid and not think about the healthy salary I had given up at my New York State job a few months earlier. But I truly loved working with the children and my fellow teachers and other school staff. I was happy there, happier than I had been for a long time.

When graduation day arrived in May I awoke and started thinking about the ceremony. Suddenly I realized that I had never picked up my tickets or cap and gown! I was in tears as I called the campus store that Saturday morning. Finally I was connected to a person who told me that the bookstore where the caps and gowns had been ordered had set up a table outside of the Convention Center. I remembered a passage from one of my daily meditation books that focused on staying calm and praying during times of trial. I trusted and prayed, put one foot in front of the other, and drove to Albany to pick up my gown and tickets. I was amazed at how smoothly the day went!

The ceremony was very moving, and I felt blessed. When I crossed the stage to get my diploma, my older son yelled "Yo, Mom!" My parents were also with us. Everyone was very proud of me, and I was pretty pleased with completing this journey successfully! I had a fine cumulative average—3.96—which validated the hard work I had invested.

After the ceremony there was a reception in the campus center, which we attended briefly. But before I could eat my fill of cookies, my husband whisked us out of there. We had planned on going out to dinner to celebrate, but he seemed to be driving in the wrong direction of the restaurant. Before I knew it, we were pulling up in front of my friend Marian's house. Everyone in the car was smiling mysteriously as we got out and walked toward the door. To my surprise, there was a party in my honor! Marian had invited a group of my good friends to celebrate my graduation. It was a lovely party and once again, I felt blessed and deeply grateful. I hadn't been given a surprise party since I was sixteen years old, and I felt about that age once again, I was so delighted! I felt humbled and very grateful that day.

In June, I came to the realization that I had spent years attempting to determine a diagnosis for my older son but it didn't really matter: what I had to deal with were the behaviors, which were the symptoms. I accepted that he had an illness that we could not cure. We could, however, learn how to cope with it, just as he could learn how to live with it. This is when I saw one of those great spiritual truths revealed: when I am able to accept something wholly and completely, it usually begins to change. Within a few months, the doctor at the intensive outpatient program tried a new medication, and he was wise enough to prescribe it in a form that melted in the mouth, so that it couldn't be removed and hidden when we left the room. Within days the personality of the boy we knew as a child began to resurface. It was pretty miraculous, almost like a resurrection. And soon we had the diagnoses, which have remained consistent since then. The medication allowed our son to settle down, get a job, get a GED, move out of our house, into a supportive housing program, and deal with the consequences of both his wise and unwise choices.

So 2001 was a year of change, in both Abba House and my house. Abba House was no longer the home of a contemplative community; it became a spiritual life center open only during hours when programs were offered. My house became more peaceful as my son began taking medication that actually addressed his illness. We still had plenty of challenges. Within a few months we began exploring an Aging Out Adolescent Program that would enable him to move out of the house and into supported housing, which benefitted all of us tremendously.

My career also changed completely, as I began seven years of teaching special education.

But that's another story.

Abba House—In Their Own Words

Kinds of Prayer
—Excerpt from program notes, Sister Mary Gen

There are many KINDS OF PRAYER. We can use what helps us most in prayer. But it is good to know about the different kinds of prayer and even to try them out if we want.

There are prayers of praise, thanksgiving, forgiveness and petition.

There is intercessory prayer, prayer for guidance, prayers of confidence.

These can be prayers from a prayer book or prayers that you make up as you go along.

These prayers can take the form of the Rosary, or the Christian prayer of the church, or the prayers at Mass.

One can pray listening to music or using body movements like dance or aerobics.

As for methods of prayer, beside those already mentioned, there is Scriptural prayer, shared prayer, Charismatic prayer, Centering Prayer, journal writing and many other forms of prayer to suit your needs.

The most important thing to remember is that God is everywhere and we can pray to God at any time, any place. We must pray like children, fully confident of a loving God. God comes to us when we least expect Him. He came to Peter in a boat; to

Matthew at his tax both at work; to Zacchaeus in a tree; to Paul while on a journey. So where is God going to come to you?

You may ask, how does one pray?

The Spirit teaches us how to pray and shows us the right way for us. Imagine yourself having a very dear friend come to visit you whom you haven't seen for a very long time. You will prepare for her by cleaning up the house and making yourself free to spend all the time you have with her. You both sit together in each other's presence, not wanting to do anything else. You keep looking at each other, not wanting to take your eyes away. You smile and feel good all over for just being there together.

What if you took out a book and began reading it? What if you began thinking of other things to do, of your work, your dinner that night or whatever, and still seemed to be listening to your friend? What if you excused yourself to go somewhere and left your friend by herself? This is what prayer is, and is not. God wants our total attention, without reading or thinking about other things.

Experience of Creation/Finding God in Nature

—Excerpt from program notes, Sister Mary Gen

Many things in nature mean much to me. I love new growth; the fidelity of nature, but most of all the things that God has made—things that no one else can make. For example, the sunrise: it not only brings light, but also shows the beauty of everything. And every twenty-four hours it appears on the horizon, without fail, ever faithful.

One of the ways to be thankful for the gifts of nature that God has given us is to use our five senses to appreciate God's gifts there.

Another part of nature that I love is the ocean. I can look out over the waters, perhaps at sunrise, and see the beauty of the sun's glow. I see the placid waters, gradually waking up and beginning to move. I listen to the seagulls, and the wind beginning to move the waters. I feel the early morning sun taking the chill off the night. I can go down to the water's edge and put my hands in the water: it is soft, cool, gentle. I could also taste it: it has the taste of salt, of fish. I try to smell the salt and the fish. I realize in all of this the hand of God who made everything, and that He loves me. I realize how much I love all of this and how much I love God. I give him thanks, and love and praise, for the beauties of his creation.

A NATURE WALK is the best way to experience the beauty of the outdoors. It leads us to thank God for his gifts and to dwell on the beauty we see.

- LOOK at everything, and then focus on one thing. Take a tree, for instance. Look at its shape, color, size, texture. Thank God for your vision, that you can see the details of this tree and everything else you look at.
- LISTEN to everything around you. Listen to the silence. Listen to the leaves rustling together, the branches moving in the wind. Listen to the birds singing and the other noises that make up the outside. Thank God for your hearing.
- TOUCH what you can around you. Touch the leaves of the tree, the branches, the trunk, and feel what the leaves are like, what the trunk feels like, whether it is hard or soft, etc. Thank God for your sense of touch. Reflect on what you do with your hands, and how many things you touch in your life.
- TASTE what you can around you. Taste the leaves if you can, or the fruit from a tree. Enjoy God's gift there.
- SMELL what you can around you. Thank God for your sense of smell, which helps you enjoy what He gives you.

By enjoying different places in nature we find God. We increase our awareness of nature and the awareness of the presence of God in the world and in ourselves when we appreciate nature. And we ask God "What are you saying to me through nature? What message are you giving me today?"

"Speak, Lord, Your Servant is Listening"
Written by Sister Libby, published in RSCJ newsletter, 1991

These words received from Sr. Marie-Louise Schroen on a "Scripture Conge'" in the noviceship have proven to be truly prophetic. For forty years God has been speaking to me clearly, unambiguously, lovingly, giving messages that are signposts on my journey. Clearly and eagerly also have I listened and heard. But to hear thoroughly is to obey (derived from "ab-audire"), and in this my record is marred with failures and "incompletes." Yet even so I hear words of mercy and forgiveness. Let me therefore share some of these "little words" as thanksgiving.

During a retreat before taking the habit I read the words: "We can give God nothing except willingness to receive everything from Him." Found in the text of a previously preached retreat by a priest whose name, I think, was Pierce, they truly unbound me from the nervous pursuit of virtues and taught me to give God the initiative in my spiritual life as well as the assessment of its progress. Later when we studied the Rule and Constitutions the passage on lively faith grabbed me; "A lively faith which impresses deeply upon them the truth that God is all and that everything else is nothing." These words explained the first message in a new way and they have been an enormous help in facing difficulties, disappointments, misunderstandings, trials and sufferings. And Marie-Louise kept saying, "There is only one way, the way of the Cross."

Aspirant years were marked by some form of spiritual darkness accompanied by a growing love of prayer even though devoid of consolation. I would ask permission for extra time in the chapel during the summer. One day I challenged God, "Why is it that you are so distant and silent when I'm trying so hard to be with you?" The answer came: "I am no longer saying things to you nor stirring your emotions because that would imply distance between you and me. Instead I am just being in you!" Several years later the words of John 14:3 lit up anew. "I shall return to take you to myself so that you may *be with me* where I am." And it became evident that we do not have to wait for death to know this experience. And again, being with Him means being on the cross at some point or points, as He was in this life.

With such a firm foundation I was able to remain fixed like a rock during those troubled transition years from 1960 to 1970 or so. At the peak of the storm, strength came through the words of Jeremiah's Lamentation #3: "It is good to wait in silence for Yahweh to save." Sister Mavie Coakly came to visit me while I was teaching in a New York City public school in Harlem and suggested Mt. Saviour Benedictine Monastery for my private retreat, a kind of innovation at the time. Then and for the next twenty years, this quiet Benedictine Monastery has been a sure refuge for me. The simple peace of a very pastoral environment has made me newly alive to God's presence again and again. In this place the words I always hear are: "On the mountain Yahweh provides" (Gen 22:14).

Time marches on, situations change, but the words of the Lord endure forever. Or maybe now it is the Word more than words, faith more than insights, the presence of Father, Son and Spirit more than phrases or sentences. Reinforcement comes in human words exchanged from time to time with "soul-friends" whom God has placed in my life at certain periods. Truly we have nothing to give God, who has everything to give us. At first He gives words and understanding, later His own being with all its fullness. Perhaps I am beginning to comprehend the Pauline words applicable since my Baptism and echoing mysteriously in my heart over all these years: "The life I live now is not my own. Christ is living in me" (Gal 2:20). Comforting indeed is the fact that this was also one of St. Madeleine Sophie's favorite passages.

BIBLIOGRAPHY

"Abba Community," Convent of the Sacred Heart, Albany, New York 12202, November 1971 (signed in C.J.M by Libby Hoye, RSCJ, Mabel Dorsey, RSCJ, Mary Gen Smyth, RSCJ, Mary L. Parkinson, Rose Marie Quilter, RSCJ).

"Abba House: An abode of faith," Kate Blain, Assistant Editor, The Evangelist, September 6, 2001.

"Abba House a wellspring for quenching spiritual thirst: Started by two sisters, now open to laity," Grace O'Connor, Albany Times Union, March 1985.

"Abba House Aims to Foster Prayer," Eric Retzlaff, Gazetter Reporter, The Schenectady Gazette, July 11, 1981.

"Abba House Celebrates 25 Years of Spiritual Ministry in Albany, NY," RSCJ Newsletter, 1976.

"Abba House Marks 10th Anniversary" RSCJ Newsletter, 1981.

"Abba House of Prayer an Ecumenical Reality," Rev. Donald Hill, The Evangelist, January 12, 1978.

Abba House of Prayer an Oasis—Only a Bus Stop Away," The Times Record, November 15, 1986.

"Abba House of Prayer is 20," Kathleen Dooley, Albany Times Union, 1991.

"Abba House of Prayer marks its 20th," David Scott, Assistant Editor, The Evangelist, November 7, 1991.

Abba House of Prayer: To and From the Center, David Steindl-Rast, OSB, delivered on the occasion of Abba House 10th Anniversary.

"Abba House of Prayer founders say goodbye," Michele Newman, The Record, Troy, NY October 7, 2001.

"Abba House puts prayer in middle of Albany city bustle," Margarette Connor, Staff Writer, The Evangelist, September 15, 1988.

"Abba House still leads community in prayer," Winifred Yu, Albany Times Union, October 5, 1996.

"Abba House: Urban Center for Prayer," Patricia Crewell, The Evangelist, November 27, 1986.

"Abba: Prayer-come-true for some in area," Bruce Scruton, Knickerbocker News, October 24, 1981.

"A house of comfort, prayer and community," Rev. Robert Limpert, The Evangelist, May 13, 1999.

"An Ecumenical Surprise," Mary Genevieve Smyth, RSCJ, RSCJ Newsletter, 1991

An Interior Spirit: Anthology of Writings of the Superiors General of the Society of the Sacred Heart, Society of the Sacred Heart, St. Louis, Mo 2000.

"A place for prayer: Nuns' vision leads to a home for quiet reflection," Grace O'Connor, Albany Times Union, April 8, 1989

"At-Home Retreat Focuses on Women, Eric Retzlaff, Gazette Reporter, The Schenectady Gazette, September 5, 1981.

"Building on Commonality," (Our Neighbor's Faith)" Elizabeth G. Hoye, RSCJ, The Evangelist, January 31, 1991.

"Catholics can study Bible as part of Lenten exercises," Kate Blain, The Evangelist, February 22, 1996.

Catholic Encyclopedia, http://www.newadvent.org/cathen/02283a.htm, January 23, 2010.

Conversation with John Arber, January 12, 2010.

Conversation with Bishop David Ball, November 11, 2009, January 19, 2010.

Conversation with Terri Bronner, March 7, 2010.

Conversation with Ann B., January 27, 2010.

Conversation with Walt Chura, September 2, 2009.

Conversation with Helene Conroy, August 30, 2009.

Conversation with Gertrude Cosenke, RSCJ, January 23, 2010.

Conversation with BJ Costello, June 5, 2009.

Conversation with Patricia Crewell, January 11, 2011.

Conversation with Rev. James Cronen, OSB, October 10, 2009.

Conversation/correspondence with Pat Doyle, January-February 2010.

Conversation with Jean Ford, RSCJ, February 10, 2010.

Conversation with Justine Guernsey, February 8, 2010.

Conversation with Deacon Barbara Hanstine, February 15, 2010.

Conversations with Betty Ann Hart, April, 2009.

Conversation with Kitt Jackson, February 16, 2010.

Conversations with Rev. James Kane, August 19, 2009; August 11, 2009.

Conversation/e-mail with Jeanne King, March, 2010.

Conversation with Bob Lamar, March 14, 2010.

Conversation with Ian Leet, November 11, 2009.

Conversation with Rev. Bob Limpert, January 19, 2010.

Conversation with Cora McLaughlin, RSCJ, January 23, 2010.

Conversation with Francis Murphy, RSCJ, January 23, 2010.

Conversation with Rev. David Noone, June 16, 2008.

Conversation with Rabbi Dan Ornstein, March 14, 2010.

Conversation with Mary Parkinson, RSCJ, January 23, 2010.

Conversations with Father Paul Roman, May 2009.

Conversation with Deacon Nancy Rosenblum, January 19, 2010.

Conversation with Carmela Richards, February 15, 2010.

Conversation with Donna Schneider, September 8, 2009.

Conversation with Mary Skinner, January 23, 2010.

Conversation with Anne Snyder, August 30, 2009.

Conversation with Bala Subramanian, February 22, 2010.

Conversation with Rev. Delos Wampler, January 16, 2010.

Correspondence with Mary Ellen Colfer, June 10, 2010.

Correspondence with Pat Doyle, February 24, 2010.

Correspondence with Father John Patrick Sullivan, May 9, 2010.

Correspondence with Anne Tekansik (Sister Libby's niece), June 27, 2009

"Ecumenical Living at Abba House: on Father, one prayer life for all," The Crux of Prayer, June 1979.

"Ecumenical Witnesses Attend Area Baptisms," Winifred Yu, Albany Times Union, December 30, 1995.

"Exploring the flowering of prayer houses," David Scott, The Evangelist, November 21, 1991.

Gimber, Frances RSCJ, "The Contemporary Society of the Sacred Heart." Text of a talk given at a meeting of Associates and Coordinators of Associates, St. Charles, Missouri, April 2, 2005.

"Hermit escapes to find God, others, self," Brian Baker,

"Houses of Prayer: Crossroads," Sister Rose Marie Quilter, RSCJ, October 1972, Abba House Archives.

<u>Happy Memories of A Saint (Les Loisirs de l'Abbaye)</u> P. Perdreau, Sands and Company 1944.

"House of Prayer marking its silver jubilee," Patricia A. Crewell, The Evangelist, October 10, 1996.

"How Our Ministry Grew," The Evangelist, October 24, 1996, Sr. Libby Hoye, RSCJ

Kilroy, Phil, <u>Madeleine Sophie Barat: A Life</u>, Paulist Press, Mahwah, NJ, 2000.

"Memories of Learning as Lambs," Lynn Callanan Gardner, The Times Union, June 11, 2011.

Obituary, Hoye, Sister Elizabeth (Libby), RSCJ, Times Union,

"On retreat with Dan Berrigan," Sally Maloy, The Evangelist, March 22, 1984.

"Prayer site seeks to continue role," Marilyn Hipp, The Schenectady Gazette, October 3, 2001.

"Recovery group has eye on God," Liz Urbanski, Staff Writer, The Evangelist, October 22, 1982.

"Scholar urges a holistic approach to Gospels," Winifred Yu, no date

"Spiritual Direction: Looking for God Sometimes Means Asking for Directions," Patricia A. Crewell, The Evangelist, November 14, 1996.

"Spotlight on a House of Prayer: Abba House of Prayer. Ecumenical living at Abba House: one Father, one prayer life for all," The Crux of Prayer, June 1979.

"Twenty-five and counting: ABBA House of Prayer instructs people in prayer," Vicki Colasurdo, Troy Record, 1976.

"Why the Sisterhood?" Libby Hoye, RSCJ RSCJ Newsletter 1991

http://www.paxchristiusa.org/about_us_history.asp, Statement of Purpose, History.

CPSIA information can be obtained at www.ICGtesting.com
Printed in the USA
BVOW07s0225081113

335716BV00002B/3/P